The Liminal Papacy of Pope Francis

Catholicity in an Evolving Universe
Ilia Delio, General Editor

This series of original works by leading Catholic figures explores all facets of life through the lens of catholicity: a sense of dynamic wholeness and a conscious awareness of a continually unfolding creation.

CATHOLICITY IN AN EVOLVING UNIVERSE

The Liminal Papacy
of Pope Francis

Moving toward Global Catholicity

M<small>ASSIMO</small> F<small>AGGIOLI</small>

ORBIS BOOKS
Maryknoll, New York 10545

Founded in 1970, Orbis Books endeavors to publish works that enlighten the mind, nourish the spirit, and challenge the conscience. The publishing arm of the Maryknoll Fathers and Brothers, Orbis seeks to explore the global dimensions of the Christian faith and mission, to invite dialogue with diverse cultures and religious traditions, and to serve the cause of reconciliation and peace. The books published reflect the views of their authors and do not represent the official position of the Maryknoll Society. To learn more about Orbis Books, please visit our website at www.orbisbooks.com.

A version of Chapter 2 ("Francis and the Reception of Vatican II as a Global Council") was previously published as "The Interpretation and Reception of Vatican II" in *Pope Francis: A Voice for Mercy, Justice, Love, and Care for the Earth*, ed. Barbara E. Wall and Massimo Faggioli (Maryknoll, NY: Orbis Books, 2019).

Given the differences in the quality of the translations into English of the conciliar documents, the quotations of conciliar documents are taken in some cases from the Vatican website; in other cases from *Vatican Council II: Constitutions, Decrees, Declarations*, edited by Austin Flannery (Northport, NY: Costello Pub. Co., 1996); and in other cases from *The Documents of Vatican II*, Walter M. Abbott, SJ, general editor, and Joseph Gallagher, translation editor (New York: America Press, 1966). The author has also made some minor changes. All official church documents are available in English on the Vatican website.

Manufactured in the United States of America

Library of Congress Cataloging-in-Publication Data

Names: Faggioli, Massimo, author. | Delio, Ilia, editor.
Title: The liminal papacy of Pope Francis : moving toward global catholicity / Massimo Faggioli, Ilia Delio, editor.
Description: Maryknoll, NY : Orbis, 2020. | Series: Catholicity in an evolving universe | Includes bibliographical references and index. | Summary: "A historical analysis of the ways in which Francis's papacy is unusual and thus open to greater possibilities than many of his predecessors" — Provided by publisher.
Identifiers: LCCN 2019035960 (print) | LCCN 2019035961 (ebook) | ISBN 9781626983687 (paperback) | ISBN 9781608338320 (ebook)
Subjects: LCSH: Papacy. | Petrine office. | Popes—Primacy. | Francis, Pope, 1936–
Classification: LCC BX1805 . F34 2020 (print) | LCC BX1805 (ebook) | DDC 282.092—dc23
LC record available at https://lccn.loc.gov/2019035960
LC ebook record available at https://lccn.loc.gov/2019035961

To my sister, Ilaria
On another shore of the global church

Fr. Bob,
Thank for welcoming me into
your luminous ministry to the Mary,
Mother of God community.
Peace and all good to
you in the future!
Your franciscan-hearted brother
+ friend !!!
Jim Burke

May 7, 2023
Fifth Sunday of Easter

Contents

Acknowledgments

The pontificate of Francis has changed the lives of many people, including Catholic theologians and scholars of the Catholic Church—from the very beginning of the pontificate up to the present. In this sense, writing a book on Francis can only be understood as part of the collective effort to comprehend this moment in the life of the Catholic community and of the human family. This book represents an attempt to systematize and deepen reflections on developments since February 2013 that are inseparable from the experience of this pontificate—an experience shared with others in the global church and in the world.

There are many fellow travelers who should be mentioned here. All over the global Catholic world some members of the Society of Jesus have, in some mystical sense, become the religious community I decided not to join when I was much younger. I want to thank here Antonio Spadaro, SJ, and the magazine he edits, *La Civiltà Cattolica* in Rome, which has been the place where very important conversations took place during the pontificate; Hans Zollner, SJ, president of the Center for Child Protection at the Pontifical Gregorian University, who has provided precious opportunities for common engagement in a very particular moment in my life as a Catholic and as a scholar; Mark Massa, SJ, director of the Boisi Center for Religion and American Public Life at Boston College, the campus where my American experience started in 2008; and John O'Malley, SJ, at Georgetown University, who embodies the kind of scholar one can only hope to imitate. In Brazil, the Jesuits at Unisinos University in São Leopoldo and at the Jesuit School of Philosophy and Theology (FAJE) in Belo Horizonte offered me cherished opportunities to share and develop some of the reflections I had during the preparation of this book.

During Francis's pontificate, my Jesuit network expanded to Australia: Mick Kelly, SJ, Gerard Goldman, and the Broken Bay Institute have opened a new world and a new vision of global Catholicity for which I will always be grateful. "Down Under" I have had incredibly enriching and entertaining moments of scholarly and friendly exchange with Archbishop Mark Coleridge, Gerald O'Collins, SJ, and Ormond Rush. In Chile, I had wonderful opportunities for exchange with Carlos Schickendantz at the Universidad Alberto Hurtado of the Jesuits in Santiago and with Sandra Arenas at Pontificia Universidad Católica de Chile.

This project became possible also thanks to Robert Mickens, a dear friend and the editor-in-chief of *La Croix International*, where I could learn a lot—and write every two weeks—about the tumultuous and extremely vital global Catholic world. But it is also true that I never really left Italy for good; my friends and colleagues at the magazines *Il Regno* and *Il Mulino* in Bologna, and *Jesus* in Milan, have kept alive the necessary lifeline of *italianità* (Italian-ness).

I am also grateful for the US vantage point of *Commonweal* magazine and the *National Catholic Reporter*, real hubs for exploring the possibilities of a non-retrograde Catholic modernity amid the disruptions of globalization and a US-centered world order.

Some friendships have been tested by the pontificate of Francis and its impact on the church; others have become stronger, among them, Gerald Beyer, Catherine Clifford, Bryan Froehle, Anthony Godzieba, Michael Hollerich, Cathleen Kaveny, Kerry Robinson, Gerald Schlabach, Matt Sitman, and Michael Sean Winters. Very special among these, on the other side of the Atlantic, is my friendship with Sr. Maria Elisa at the Monastery of Ara Crucis in Faenza, Italy, who always tests my impressions of the world beyond the cloister. And the ecumenical monastic community of Bose, Italy, is more than ever a reference point for framing the issue of the globalization of Christianity, with a solid anchoring in the spiritual and theological tradition preceding the second millennium and the Westernization of Catholicism. In this sense the book is also a product of the reflections exchanged in the global network of scholars working on a new intercontinental commentary of Vatican II, thanks to the initiative of Margit

Eckholt; Joachim Schmiedl; and my German mentor, professor emeritus at the University of Tübingen, Peter Hünermann.

Last but not least, I want to thank my department colleague Ilia Delio and Orbis Books for including this book in the Catholicity in an Evolving Universe series. My editor at Orbis, Jill O'Brien, has followed this project very closely, in all its stages, with great care and even greater patience with the author of the book.

I am also thankful for the many opportunities I have had to contribute to the larger intra-Catholic conversation—in different areas of the world and beyond the academic community, this Italian and European member of the Catholic Church became more fully Catholic—and to learn from my American wife and our children how to negotiate Italian and American Catholic roots, while the Atlantic was becoming wider from both a political and an ecclesial standpoint. This book is an integral part of my experience of being Catholic in the very particular time and place that is the United States of America during the pontificate of Pope Francis.

Foreword

ILIA DELIO

The aim of the Catholicity in an Evolving Universe series from Orbis Books is to understand how the evolution of Catholic thought and doctrine is taking place in a world of increasing complexity. *Evolution* is a word seldom used to describe the papacy and is usually reserved for particular discussions in science and religion. But it is an appropriate word to describe this new book by Massimo Faggioli, a leading church historian and an expert on the papacy of Pope Francis. The pontificate of Francis can be described as a papacy in evolution. History has become too complex to convey via a linear narrative, Faggioli contends, and must be assessed according to a complexity of factors, which include the global, universal, and local dimensions of the Catholic Church. This new book examines the pontificate of Pope Francis from a three-dimensional view, taking a postmodern approach to understanding the church and the papacy by viewing the church as a subject in the midst of shifting narratives.

Faggioli's book provides a masterful treatment of the church in the modern era, as it finds itself amid the forces of globalization, religious pluralism, and scientific thinking. Rather than a purely historical description of Jorge Bergoglio's ascent to the papacy, we are provided with a rich, multi-textured narrative that describes a relationship between the person Jorge Bergoglio, the conditions in which he emerged as the successor to Pope Emeritus Benedict XVI, and the shifting context of his papacy in light of Vatican II. With Bergoglio, we have a pope from the southern hemisphere assuming leadership in the Catholic Church at a particular historical moment following Vatican II and the unusual retirement of Benedict XVI, and leading the church in radically new ways. His papacy is at once personal, historical, and contextual, all of which are discussed, as the church evolves from a Western hegemonic force to a global Catholic Church that must find its way in a world of increasing complexity. What shines through is the way Pope Francis draws his inspiration from the gospel of Jesus Christ and a grounding of the gospel in history. Francis is deeply concerned with the transformative power of the gospel, and his deep trust in a living God who is the ground and source of all life is not to be underestimated.

This book offers the reader a wealth of knowledge and insight on the complexities of Pope Francis's papacy. Faggioli opens new windows in the ecclesiology of globalization and illuminates the significance of Francis's creative leadership amid the struggles of globalization as he shapes the church for a new role in the world. The papacy of Pope Francis is unfinished, Faggioli reminds us, and new challenges and opportunities for the growth of the church in the twenty-first century must continue to be explored.

Pope Francis and Global Catholic History

Historicization and Periodization: The Liminality of Francis's Pontificate

Writing and speaking about Pope Francis from a historical point of view during his pontificate is understandably difficult. It is challenging to discuss any pope and any pontificate, but it is even more so in a church now dominated more than it used to be by mass media, digital and social media, and a news cycle without gatekeepers and often without editorial control. The immediacy—temporal and otherwise—of the new information environment has to be reconciled with the long-term perspective of Catholic institutional culture and the long duration of the tectonic movements within Catholicism as a social and cultural entity.

Addressing Pope Francis's pontificate from a historical perspective is complicated. It is an unfinished pontificate at the time of completing this book (in fact, a pontificate in full swing). But there is also a more complex issue at the heart of Francis's papacy. For a long time Francis's pontificate has been viewed almost as if it were hanging in the vacuum between the sudden end of the previous pontificate and the beginning of his own pontificate. There has been an "unfinished transition" from one pontificate to another, because of Pope Benedict XVI's decision to resign, to become emeritus (a title that did not exist before and is theologically and canonically questionable) and to live in the Vatican as emeritus in conditions that are not dramatically different from when he was pope.

But there is a deeper liminality at the heart of this pontificate. The first liminal aspect of Francis's papacy has to do with the way Jorge Mario Bergoglio became pope, inaugurating a pontificate while his predecessor's was not completely over in the eyes of the global church—Francis on the threshold between the old and the new.

The conclave that elected Francis in 2013 took place in an extraordinary situation: as Francis's predecessor not only prepared but also survived the conclave, one could say that in some sense the conclave of 2013 never really ended. The conclave is a juridical-ritual way for the institution and the community to process "the killing of the father": the deceased pope joins the line of predecessors, and the new pope is given institutional and charismatic powers. But as we know, the election of Francis took place in a very different situation. Hence the difficult reception of Francis's pontificate and the difficulty of writing history about it in a church where the transition between pontificates—when accomplished with the death of the pope—tends to settle old intellectual, personal, and "corporate" scores, and also to redefine individual and collective loyalties. The transition of Benedict XVI from pope to pope emeritus has left in the church and in theology "outstanding bills" that a normal transition between pontificates tend to resolve in a much shorter period of time.

Church historians cannot ignore this particularity in the ecclesial environment surrounding Francis's pontificate, because the place of a pontificate in history is not immune to the reception of the pontificate's development. Despite the canonical definition of Francis as pope since March 13, 2013, we cannot really say that in the perception of Catholics the pontificate of his predecessor, Benedict XVI, ended completely on the day designated by Benedict XVI, that is, February 28, 2013, at 8:00 p.m. local time in Rome.

In other words, there is a liminality to Francis's papacy that begins with his very election in the conclave and symbolizes the entire pontificate and its meaning for global Catholicism: a key junction in the history of the Catholic Church between an "already" and a "not yet" that can be understood only by analyzing this pontificate from a multilayered historical perspective.

At the same time, when writing about a pope, one must remember that Christianity is history *and* geography. This is particularly true for Francis's pontificate. The liminality of Francis is at the same time historical and geographical. His emphasis on the margin and the peripheries entails also a redefinition of boundaries and borders. Francis is a pope from the margins, visibly challenging the revival of the borders in our political discourse. In Francis's imagination the border is more a *limen* (threshold) than a *limes* (rigid frontier). The concept of liminality is key to understanding Francis's pontificate because of his reinterpretation of the borders in this age of new walls. It's a border that relates and connects the "other" more than it excludes. This is at the heart of Francis's project, in which liminality is a central aspect of the *pontifex*, etymologically the "bridge builder," both *geographically*—in his focus on a new map of the global world in the disruption of globalization, and *historically*—in his efforts to reconnect the church and tradition in a non-traditionalist way.

History, Pontificates, and the Church

The historic nature of the transition between Benedict XVI and Francis was partly related to the influence of a post-historical and, to a large extent, anti-historical way of understanding the church. One of the critical elements in the reception of Francis's pontificate is thus a difficulty in understanding Catholicism and the papacy in its sociocultural and institutional dimensions in historical terms—in a long-term perspective that is both backward and forward. This, in turn, is part of a larger crisis connected to the role of history in the cultural canon of Western Christianity.

On one hand, the historical element is exploited by a socially weakened Catholicism for the enhancement of the ecclesiastical historical patrimony that tends toward "monumentalization" and "musealization"; Rome and the Vatican are often reduced by current Catholic culture—including "militant" Catholicism—to a romantic backdrop feeding the aesthetic superiority complex of Catholicism over other Christian traditions, over other religious traditions, and over a secularized modernity perceived to be both morally and aesthetically lost in postmodernity. On the other hand, there is an alienation between history and theology that is found, for example, in seminary curricula. This alienation is particularly evident in some contexts, such as the North American one, in which theological studies—both for candidates to the priesthood and for lay theologians—continually reduce the emphasis on the study of the history of the church, retaining only the study of the life of saints and patristics.[1]

In both Catholic and secular academic circles, studies of church history and Christianity have to deal with the wave of social and cultural studies that minimizes the importance of historical studies for understanding the religious phenomenon. History is reduced to a narrative with a declared ideological purpose: to serve the identity of a specific group from which the narrative springs and to which it is addressed. It seems that it has become much more difficult to write about history—even the history of the church—in the way Rowan Williams described doing so a few years ago:

> The very effort to make any kind of historical narrative can be seen as a sort of act of faith, faith that massive disruption does not in fact destroy the possibilities of understanding, and thus the possibility of a shared world across gulfs of difference . . . the idea of history itself as a moral or spiritual undertaking, which gives us grounds for assuming it is possible to share a world with strangers.[2]

These gulfs of difference are even more important in the church of today for understanding Francis's pontificate, in a time when history and church history are not really part of the debate, and in a global church where a new emphasis on the local dimension often means a church overwhelmed by obsessively idiosyncratic political and cultural narratives.

The reception of Francis's pontificate cannot be properly considered without exploring the global, universal, and local

---

[1] See Katarina Schuth, *Seminary Formation: Recent History, Current Circumstances, New Directions* (Collegeville, MN: Liturgical Press, 2016).

[2] Rowan Williams, *Why Study the Past? The Quest for the Historical Church* (Grand Rapids, MI: Eerdmans, 2005), 10.

dimensions of the recent history of the Catholic Church. For example, the ecclesiological dispute around the year 2000 between Cardinal Walter Kasper and Cardinal Joseph Ratzinger reflected the tense relationship between the church's local and universal dimensions.[3] Today, the work of Catholic theologians has become less and less important to many Catholic leaders (such as bishops, public intellectuals, and major donors), who have turned their attention away from the teachings of Francis's pontificate and toward initiatives that address the "culture wars" between so-called liberals and conservatives. Because of the left-right split that had widened during the pontificate of John Paul II, many Catholics, including intellectuals and even academics, now wrote theology off as a discipline corrupted by "liberal opinion." History and church history are eminent victims of this involution, which has thus had an impact not only on the way one writes about a pope, but also on the way this particular pope is seen by his contemporaries.

Chronology and Periodization of Francis's Pontificate

From the point of view of the global Catholic Church there is no alternative to seeing Pope Francis through the lens of church history. When we talk about the issue of understanding Francis historically, we must consider the compatibility between the need to understand the church as a subject and the tendency to deconstruct the history of institutions (including church institutions and the papacy) into a series of stories and narratives centered on ever narrower fields defined by membership and by an identity that is exclusive and competitive with other identities. It seems clear that the future of historical and theological studies on the church will have to articulate in a new way the relationship between a classical approach to church history (which is less and less practiced in the academy, even in Catholic universities) and the methodological contribution of the postmodern focus on

---

[3] See Kilian McDonnell, "The Ratzinger/Kasper Debate: The Universal Church and Local Churches," *Theological Studies* 63 (2002): 227–49.

deconstruction of the institutional dimension. Postmodernity is largely abandoning the history of the church in favor of other stories or narratives of a secularist, antireligious, or a-religious tendency. In this sense trying to understand Francis's pontificate in history and in a chronological periodization can be seen as passe and irrelevant. But the attempt is necessary, provided that we go beyond the approach of a purely ecclesiastical history while also refraining from cornering ourselves in a sociocultural approach alone. The theological culture of the institutional church is not immune to the rise of the "post-truth" culture in which we now live. One of the effects of that culture may be seen in the use in church polemics—including at high levels of the ecclesiastical echelon—of a very simplified hermeneutics of "continuity and reform" versus "discontinuity and rupture" in the interpretation of Vatican II. Given this era of epistemological ambiguity, historical study has become even more crucial for understanding the development of tradition. For example, the current wave of Catholic neo-traditionalism, especially in the United States, reflects a failure to keep a healthy sense of history alive in the church. Moreover, the tendency to privilege narratives instead of history is a symptom of the politicization and privatization of history.[4] From this point of view, periodization is a useful and necessary alternative to the dominance of ideological narratives.

I propose two kinds of periodization for understanding Francis's pontificate: (1) a periodization that attempts to look at a multi-framework historical picture (ecclesiastical, theological, and global) in order to locate Francis's pontificate in different kinds of histories, an approach that is particularly necessary in the context of a pontificate of the world church;[5] and (2) an internal periodization of Francis's pontificate that analyzes the shifts within the pontificate.

---

[4] See Massimo Faggioli, "Vatican II: The History and the Narratives," *Theological Studies* 73, no. 4 (December 2012): 749–67.

[5] See Massimo Faggioli, *Pope Francis: Tradition in Transition* (Mahwah, NJ: Paulist Press, 2015), 1–19.

A Multi-Framework Periodization

There are seven frameworks we must consider for this approach: (1) the history of the Roman papacy; (2) the history of the Roman Catholic Church; (3) the history of the reception and application of Vatican II; (4) the history of theology and of the theological tradition; (5) the history of the ecclesiastical institutions; (6) the shift from a European-centered to a global church history; and (7) the global political and social history.

The History of the Roman Papacy

Francis is the first Latin American pope and the first Jesuit pope. He is also the first pope in the last century (except for the very short pontificate of John Paul I) who does not come from a career in the diplomatic service or from a professional academic background. Francis is an outsider, both to the academic and curial circles of papal Rome and to the circles of Italian Catholicism; this means that he has a particularly obvious detachment from both Italian politics and Italian church politics. Francis is also the first pope to reassess the relationship between the papacy and synodality, both in the Synod of Bishops and in the life of the church more generally. He is the first pope who is not afraid to side with the poor in a programmatic way from within the Roman Catholic Church and to advocate a "poor church" and a "church for the poor," thus challenging a series of assumptions about the relationship among Catholicism, the papacy, and the sociopolitical status quo. His contributions to the history of the papal ministry are particularly evident in his desacralization of the person of the pope; his emphasis on a new, less argumentative relationship with modernity;[6] and his foregrounding of the experience of the poor in the church. As the first pope from Latin America, Francis continues to interpret his pontificate in unprecedented ways,[7] it becomes increasingly clear that this

---

[6] See Daniele Menozzi, *I papi e il moderno. Una lettura del cattolicesimo contemporaneo (1903–2016)* (Brescia: Morcelliana, 2016), 148–59.

[7] See Alberto Melloni, *Il Giubileo. Una storia* (Roma-Bari: Laterza, 2015), 109–11.

papacy will be considered a pivotal moment in the history of global Catholicism.

The History of the Roman Catholic Church

Another helpful framework for understanding Francis's pontificate is the history of the Roman Catholic Church and in particular the relations between the pope and the councils convened since the sixteenth-century Council of Trent.[8] Francis is a pope who embodies the theology and the church of Vatican II Catholicism, but he is also a postconciliar pope with an unproblematic relationship with both the council and the postconciliar period. Furthermore, beyond the shallow controversies about the alleged liberalism or conservatism of Vatican II and the popes of the post–Vatican II period, Francis's pontificate is part of the bigger question of whether Vatican II was merely the end of the Tridentine period, opening toward a time of transition yet to be seen, or if it was the beginning of a new era in Roman Catholicism. Within this larger debate the more particular question is whether Francis is part of the ending of the Tridentine model, or of the beginning of a new period.[9] The infrequency of direct, textual mentions of Vatican II by a post–Vatican II pope like Francis is not indicative of his dismissal of the council. On the contrary, more than fifty years after Vatican II the church has reached a point in the reception of the council at which the conciliar trajectories no longer need to be labeled.[10]

---

[8] See John W. O'Malley, *Vatican I: The Council and the Making of the Ultramontane Church* (Cambridge, MA: Belknap Press of Harvard University Press, 2018), esp. 55–95 (on the Ultramontane movement in the first half of the nineteenth century).

[9] See Paolo Prodi, *Il paradigma tridentino. Un'epoca della storia della Chiesa* (Brescia: Morcelliana, 2010); idem, "Europe in the Age of Reformations: The Modern State and Confessionalization," *Catholic Historical Review* 103, no. 1 (Winter 2017): 1–19.

[10] See Massimo Faggioli, *A Council for the Global Church: Receiving Vatican II in History* (Minneapolis: Fortress Press, 2015), 329–35.

The History of the Reception and Application of Vatican II

In contrast to his predecessors' approaches to the relationship between the council and the postconciliar era, Francis embodies the shift toward a theology shaped by pastorality. As Christoph Theobald observes, "Vatican II can be defined as a 'pastoral council.' The reception of the council today means shifting towards a new stage of reception, that is, putting into practice the praxis of the council and discovering the 'conciliar pastorality' that marks that ecclesial praxis."[11] And, unlike Benedict XVI, Francis sees a consistency between Vatican II and the post–Vatican II period—his defense of the council does not require him to distance himself from the tumultuous postconciliar period. Francis also does not contrapose pre–Vatican II theological *ressourcement*, John XXIII's conciliar *aggiornamento*, and post–Vatican II (especially Paul VI's) renewal.[12] Above all, he understands the application of the council largely in terms of its reception by the local churches, which are to have a more pronounced role.

The History of Theology and of the Theological Tradition

Francis's complex assessment of modernity includes a rebalancing of the neo-Thomist and neo-Augustinian approaches to reality, following Joseph A. Komonchak's interpretation of the deep theological dynamism of Vatican II.[13] There is a philosophical divide not only between neo-Augustinians (philosophically close to Platonism) and neo-Thomists (philosophically close to

---

[11] Christoph Theobald, *Accéder à la source*, vol. 1 in *La réception du concile Vatican II* (Paris: Cerf, 2009), 886.

[12] See Serena Noceti, "What Structures Are Needed for a Reform of the Church?" in *Concilium* 2018/4: *The Church of the Future*, ed. Thierry-Marie Courau, Stefanie Knauss, and Enrico Galavotti (London: SCM Press, 2019), 85–99, esp. 96.

[13] See Joseph A. Komonchak, "Augustine, Aquinas, or the Gospel *sine glossa*?" in *Unfinished Journey: The Church Forty Years after Vatican II, Essays for John Wilkins*, ed. Austen Ivereigh (New York: Continuum, 2005), 102–18.

Aristotelians), but also between the role of theology as patristic-monastic and Augustinian versus neo-Thomistic. There is also an ecclesiological divide. As Ormond Rush notes, "The Augustinian school is wanting to set church and world in a situation of rivals; it sees the world in a negative light; evil and sin so abound in the world that the church should be always suspicious and distrustful of it. Any openness to the world would be 'naive optimism.'"[14] Francis does not see the church as far removed from a sinful world—"the Church as an island of grace in a world given over to sin," in the words of Avery Dulles[15]—but perceives deeply the "signs of the times" (Marie-Dominique Chenu),[16] the historic-ity of the church (Yves Congar),[17] and its identity as a "world church" (Karl Rahner's *Weltkirche*).[18]

The History of the Ecclesiastical Institutions

Francis's efforts to reform the Curia are significantly different from those of his predecessors. He is neither trying to achieve reform through apostolic constitutions like those of Paul VI (in 1967) and John Paul II (in 1988), for example, nor is he emulating Benedict XVI's attempt to strengthen Rome's authority in the global Catholic Church. In contrast, Francis tends to seek guidance on reform from those outside the Curia, as when he established a Council of Cardinals in 2013 that included only

---

[14] See Ormond Rush, *Still Interpreting Vatican II: Some Hermeneutical Principles* (Mahwah, NJ: Paulist Press, 2004), 15.

[15] Avery Dulles, "The Reception of Vatican II at the Extraordinary Synod of 1985," in *The Reception of Vatican II*, ed. Giuseppe Alberigo, Jean-Pierre Jossua, and Joseph A. Komonchak (Washington, DC: Catholic University of America Press, 1987), 353.

[16] See Marie-Dominique Chenu, *Vatican II Notebook*, ed. Alberto Melloni, trans. Paul Philibert (Adelaide: ATF, 2015).

[17] See Yves Congar, *True and False Reform in the Church* (Collegeville, MN: Liturgical Press, 2011), original in French, *Vraie et fausse réforme dans l'Église* (Paris: Cerf, 1950, 1968).

[18] See Karl Rahner, "Basic Theological Interpretation of the Second Vatican Council," in Karl Rahner, *Concern for the Church* (New York: Crossroad, 1981), 77–90, original in German, "Theologische Grundinterpretation des II. Vatikanischen Konzils," *Zeitschrift für katholische Theologie* 101 (1979): 290–99.

one member of the Curia and a number of people known to be critical of the way the Vatican operated. This kind of outreach is a typical aspect of Francis's pontificate, along with impulses toward a decentralization of Catholicism—a move by Francis that should for now be termed initial, open-ended, and possibly subject to reversal in the near future by another pope. Clearly Francis acknowledges the need for a new kind of role for Rome in the twentieth century (part of the solution of the "Roman question" after the end of the Papal States) together with a new awareness of both the local and global Catholic Church. Recognition of the polar tensions of *globalization* and *localization* have long been visible in the intellectual history of Jorge Mario Bergoglio.[19]

The Shift from a European-Centered to a Global Church History

The most notable change in this framework is the way Francis talks about the relationship among Europe and the Catholic Church and Christianity. He doesn't see the essential connection between the destiny of Christianity in Europe and the future of the Catholic Church upheld by John Paul II and especially by Benedict XVI. Instead, Francis believes that the Greek-Latin paradigm should play a proper but not exclusive role in a church that seeks a truly universal catholicity. This is not only because the appropriation of that Greek-Latin paradigm by the Catholic churches of Western Europe and North America is questionable, especially if understood as an appropriation exclusive of other cultural and linguistic canons within global Catholicism, but also because inclusivity should be welcomed rather than feared. As he notes in the programmatic document of his pontificate, the apostolic exhortation *Evangelii Gaudium*, "We would not do justice to the logic of the incarnation if we thought of Christianity as monocultural and monotonous," and then warns that "the message that we proclaim always has a certain cultural dress, but

---

[19] See Massimo Borghesi, *The Mind of Pope Francis: Jorge Mario Bergoglio's Intellectual Journey*, trans. Barry Hudock (Collegeville, MN: Liturgical Press, 2018), original in Italian, *Jorge Mario Bergoglio. Una biografia intellettuale* (Milan: Jaca Book, 2017), 19–55.

we in the church can sometimes fall into a needless hallowing of our own culture, and thus show more fanaticism than true evangelizing zeal" (no. 117). Francis thus elaborates the issue of Eurocentrism in a way that differs significantly from Benedict XVI's Regensburg lecture of September 12, 2006, in which Benedict lifts up the "inner rapprochement between biblical faith and Greek philosophical entity," even going so far as to seemingly back the claim that "the critically purified Greek heritage forms an integral part of Christian faith."[20] There is in Francis a very clear connection between the pastoral constitution of Vatican II, *Gaudium et Spes*, and his own document, *Evangelii Gaudium*.

Francis's pragmatism also affects his views on the trajectory of the European project: his critique of the technocratic paradigm (especially in the encyclical *Laudato Si'*) reveals him to be a critical and disenchanted supporter of the European Union (in light of the shift of the spirit of the European Union away from its origins, which were inspired in part by Catholic social teaching, and toward the technocracy of the neoliberal age). The same can be said about Francis's relations with the political and cultural center of the twentieth century, the United States, which Francis does not credit with the providential role some Americans and American Catholics presume to hold.

Global Political and Social History

This pontificate is the first to witness a clear crisis of globalization: Brexit and the election of Donald Trump in 2016 have given the pontificate a role that is different, for example, from John Paul II's fight against communism or Benedict XVI's responsibilities in a post-9/11 world.[21] Then there is the issue of the relationship between the post–Vatican II church and the globalization of Catholicism with respect to global history. The explosion of the sexual-abuse crisis in the church as a world

---

[20] For a comparison between Benedict XVI and his predecessor regarding the relationship between faith and cultures (plural), see John Paul II, *Fides et Ratio*, September 14, 1998, esp. nos. 3 and 70–72.

[21] For a historical-political analysis of the crisis of globalization, see Vittorio Emanuele Parsi, *Titanic. Il naufragio dell'ordine liberale* (Bologna: Il Mulino, 2018).

problem is also an integral part of the narrative on the globalization of Catholicism and an integral part of the history of Francis's pontificate.

The application of a global historical framework to his pontificate is necessary not just from an internal Catholic perspective on globalization, considering the impact on the church of enormous scientific, cultural, and ethical changes (for example, the emergence of bio-politics) in the differentiation between the Western world and the so-called global south. It is also needed from a church-world perspective; what was typical of the link between conciliar theology and the historical-political moments of the past (the end of colonial empires and decolonization, the de-Europeanization of Catholicism, the Cold War) must now be reconsidered in a deeply changed situation.[22] The shift from a Western world inspired by the election of Barack Obama in 2008 to the polarized era following the election of Donald Trump in 2016 is a key factor for the historical periodization of Francis's pontificate and must also be considered in a global theological-political periodization of his pontificate and its reception.

An Internal Periodization

This multi-framework attempt to understand Francis's role in history must be supplemented by another periodization, internal to the pontificate, that explores different phases and moments in Francis's tenure since his election.

Francis and Benedict's Extended Papacy

One key element to consider is the relationship between Francis's pontificate and that of Benedict XVI. First of all, there was the particular experience in the first two conclaves of the twenty-first century. Cardinal Jorge Mario Bergoglio was the runner-up

---

[22] See Stephen R. Schloesser, "'Dancing on the Edge of the Volcano': Biopolitics and What Happened after Vatican II," in *From Vatican II to Pope Francis: Charting a Catholic Future*, ed. Paul Crowley, 3–26 (Maryknoll, NY: Orbis Books, 2014).

to Cardinal Joseph Ratzinger in 2005[23] before being elected pope, rather swiftly as is typical of contemporary papal history, in the following conclave of 2013. There seems to be between Jorge Mario Bergoglio and Joseph Ratzinger a rather interesting relationship that began in 2005; it is a relationship that has developed over time, and it has been largely shielded from the public eye except for some carefully staged photo opportunities.

Indeed, both (a) the March 2018 incident in which Benedict XVI declined the invitation to write an introduction for a series of Vatican-published volumes on Francis's theology,[24] and (b) the April 2019 publication of Benedict XVI's article on the sexual abuse crisis,[25] revealed something of the complexity of the periodization of a pontificate in the age of the new institution of the "pope emeritus." The issue of the relationship between the pope and the pope emeritus has often been framed in terms of the personal loyalty of the living emeritus to the new pope—something that has never been in doubt since the latter's election in March 2013. However, the bigger and more complicated issue is the symbolical legitimacy of the new pope vis-à-vis the pope emeritus in a church where the papal ministry has become less institutional and more charismatic.

Benedict XVI's office and ministry as bishop of Rome and pope ceased on February 28, 2013, at 8 p.m. Rome time. There are some who are not fully aware of this, surprisingly also among those who want to support Pope Francis by trying to extract from the predecessor unnecessary public statements about the supposedly perfect continuity with his successor. This attempt to defend Pope Francis on the basis of the statements of Benedict XVI has created a dangerous precedent and does not come without caveats and costs, including the endless interpretations of Francis's pontificate as being in "continuity or discontinuity" with his predecessor.

---

[23] See Lucio Brunelli, "Così eleggemmo papa Ratzinger," *Limes* 4 (2005): 291–300.

[24] See Andrea Tornielli, "Viganò's Resignation: Background and Unanswered Questions," *Vatican Insider*, March 22, 2018.

[25] See Massimo Faggioli, "Benedict's Untimely Meditation: How the Pope Emeritus's Disappointing Essay on Sex Abuse Is Being Weaponized," *Commonweal* (April 12, 2019).

Whatever the institutionalization of the papacy tried to control in the charismatization of the papal role since the First Vatican Council of 1869–1870 (the declarations on papal primacy and papal infallibility), the papacy embodies now a power more charismatic than it used to be, and more charismatic than institutional. All the institutional powers of the papacy have been transferred to Francis, but not all of its charismatic powers. To paraphrase what has been written about the first black president of the United States, Barack Obama, "until there was a black presidency it was impossible to conceive of the limitations of one,"[26] we can say that until there was a pope emeritus, it was impossible to conceive of the limitations that the pope emeritus could create for the actual pope. In this sense the effort to build a periodization of Francis's pontificate cannot ignore the periodization of what can be called the extended pontificate of Benedict XVI, a post-resignation papacy made possible by the hyper-mediatization of Roman Catholicism.

Francis's Plan and Vision

To understand the role of the pope in an age in which church politics are influenced by modern mass media, one has to question the relationship between the agenda of the conclave (and the pre-conclave official and unofficial meetings) and the agenda of the pope the conclave elects.[27]

On the one hand, Francis seemingly received a mandate from the conclave (to which Francis referred in some interviews after his election) to stabilize the central government of the Catholic

---

[26] Jelani Cobb, "The Matter of Black Lives," *The New Yorker* (March 14, 2016).

[27] If the age of mass media has changed the papacy, it is time to consider how social media have changed the making of the pope and church politics in general. The role of social media during the two bishops' synods of 2014 and 2015 and in the preparation of the bishops' synod on the youth of 2018 have been instructive. See Mario Marazziti, *I papi di carta: nascita e svolta dell'informazione religiosa da Pio XII a Giovanni XXIII* (Genoa: Marietti, 1990); Federico Ruozzi, *Il concilio in diretta. Il Vaticano II e la televisione tra informazione e partecipazione* (Bologna: Il Mulino, 2012).

Church after the crisis under Benedict XVI and to reform the Roman Curia. Francis interpreted that mandate in a rather expanded and surprising way. Francis's decision to call a two-step bishops' synod on family and marriage, announced seven months after his election, is an interesting parallel with John XXIII's surprising decision to call the Second Vatican Council just three months after his election. But Francis's interpretation of his pontificate—as one that goes way beyond the agenda of a law-and-order pope who is focused on the management of the bureaucracy—was evident in the first few weeks, with his emphasis on God's mercy and a non-ideological, more welcoming Catholicism. If the conclave elected Jorge Mario Bergoglio on the basis of a specific plan, it now seems clear that Francis had other plans.

The presence of the pope emeritus in the Vatican has created some constraints for Francis's pontificate, however, in terms of reconciling his own plans with those of his predecessor. Unlike the situation in which Paul VI dutifully took up the task of resuming the Second Vatican Council, which had been suspended by the death of John XXIII in June 1963, there was extraordinary pressure from the beginning of Francis's pontificate for him to signal an institutional, formal continuity with his living predecessor and his unfinished business. Francis did specifically address the goals and hopes of Benedict XVI in the encyclical *Lumen Fidei* of June 2013 (especially in its introductory paragraphs) and then expressed his own concerns much more fully in the apostolic exhortation *Evangelii Gaudium* of November 2013.

To be sure, *Evangelii Gaudium* is an apostolic exhortation that follows the bishops' synod of 2012 on evangelization, but it is really the theological vision of Francis for his pontificate and is more directly linked to Bergoglio's leadership in the Latin American church (the fifth conference of Latin American bishops in Aparecida, May 2007) than to the 2012 synod. It is a settled conclusion that *Evangelii Gaudium* represents Francis's long-term vision for the church, stemming from an original interpretation of Vatican II that is distinct from that of John Paul II or Benedict XVI. But *Evangelii Gaudium* can also be seen as a development of the ecclesiological vision of *Gaudium et Spes* from the model of a sphere to a polyhedron expressive of Francis's complex understanding of the church in globalization.[28] In this sense *Evangelii Gaudium* represents the formal announcement of the theology of the pontificate, and it thus has a periodizing value.

The Synodal Event of 2014–2015 and Amoris Laetitia

But *Evangelii Gaudium* is not the center of Francis's pontificate from the point of view of either its chronology or significance. On October 8, 2013, Pope Francis announced that in October 2014 there would be an extraordinary general assembly of the synod of bishops on topics related to the family and evangelization. Subsequent communications made clear that the extraordinary general assembly would be followed by an ordinary general assembly of the synod of bishops in October 2015 on the same topics. The celebration of the two synods was followed on April 8, 2016, by the post-synodal apostolic exhortation *Amoris Laetitia*, which is a result of Francis's reflection on the discussions and outcomes of both synods.

My contention is that the twin synods of October 2014 (extraordinary synod) and October 2015 (ordinary synod) on the same topic (a first in the postconciliar history of the Catholic Church) occupy a central place in Francis's pontificate. The synodal experience of 2014 and 2015, and by extension from the announcement in the fall of 2013 to the publication of *Amoris Laetitia* in April 2016, represents the significant pivot point of the pontificate. Francis's leadership style and mission in the church had already become clear in the early months of his pontificate. But it was between the end of 2013 (after the announcement of the two synods) and April 2016 (with the publication of *Amoris Laetitia*) that Francis made his main argument to the church and to the world. In a sense, what Vatican II was for John XXIII, the synodal event was for Francis, both from a *theological* standpoint (how to understand the pontificate's relationship to the gospel and the tradition) and a *historical* standpoint (what took place).

---

[28] See Christoph Theobald, "L'exhortation apostolique *Evangelii Gaudium*. Esquisse d'une interprétation originale du Concile Vatican II," *Revue Théologique de Louvain* 46 (2015): 321–40, esp. 337–39.

This choice of the bishops' synods of 2014 and 2015 as the center of Francis's pontificate is not motivated by the attention they gave to particular issues—especially in relation to divorced and remarried Catholics—but rather because in that synodal event we can see many elements typical of Francis's pontificate, in some sense even a summation of his theological vision:

- *A church that goes forth to reach those in "irregular situations"*: What Francis started to say from the beginning of his pontificate about the need to break away from a moralistic understanding of Christianity found full expression in the synodal discussions around the complexity of moral judgments on issues of love, family, and marriage.
- *A church that is not afraid to address issues that for some had been settled forever just a few years before*: Francis's efforts at resuming the discourse on Vatican II and the development of the tradition did not remain abstract but faced head on the challenge of reassessing the adequacy of the church's language on new issues; this was especially courageous given that he was operating in a moment in church history marked by the resurgence of neo-traditionalist and neo-fundamentalist tendencies.
- *A church that is aware and honest about the tensions between the law and the gospel*: In the corpus of Vatican II there seems to be no discernable tension among *ius, iustitia*, and *misericordia*. This can be interpreted as part of the council's attempt to give credit to earthly realities, as well as to the church's witness for the progress of justice in this world. In *Gaudium et Spes* the idea of justice is articulated in terms of social, economic, and international justice, looking at the possible applicability of Catholic social doctrine to the political realm. It is part of the positive view of Vatican II on the world—positive in the sense of a still-limited awareness of the complex relationship and tensions among the law, the gospel, and the world. In contrast, Francis's take on the relationship between law and gospel is more pragmatic and less optimistic.
- *A church that recognizes the need for a renewed collegial and synodal dimension*: Francis's decision to call the two synods and the way he led the synodal event are part of

his assessment of the successes and the failures of the post–Vatican II institutional church to keep the promise made by the council in terms of a more participatory ecclesial community. His speech of October 17, 2015, for the fiftieth anniversary of the institution of the Synod of Bishops, is the most important speech of a pope to date on the issue, the papal *magna carta* of synodality.

- *A church that faces the complexity of its global dimension, where the issue of unity in diversity takes different shape than it has in the recent past:* Tensions around different theological and cultural comprehensions of new issues (such as homosexuality, divorce, polygamy, and premarital cohabitation) surfaced during the two synods of 2014 and 2015 as never before in an official gathering of bishops in the Vatican. Pope Francis made it possible for these differences to emerge, to be on full display, and to be part of the process of synthesis at the synod, both in his papal reception of the synod (as seen in *Amoris Laetitia*) and in the ecclesial reception of the synod.

Francis's view of the relationship between the magisterium and the people of the church shaped the whole synodal experience: from the questionnaires before the opening of the synod, to the relations between the synod and the media, to the understanding of the role of *Amoris Laetitia* as a papal document offered to a synodal reception by the church.

From a strictly historical point of view this post-synodal exhortation played a unique role in the reception of Francis's pontificate. The aftermath of the synod and the publication of *Amoris Laetitia* in April 2016 revealed several key elements of his pontificate.

One of these elements is the deepening, narrowing, and extremization of the opposition to Francis from 2016 in particular areas and circles of the church. On September 13, 2016, Francis wrote a letter to the bishops of Argentina (region of Buenos Aires) praising their pastoral solution for divorced and remarried Catholics (one of the issues he had addressed in *Amoris Laetitia*). Yet a letter critical of *Amoris Laetitia* was submitted that year by four cardinals (Carlo Caffarra, archbishop emeritus of Bologna; Raymond Burke, patron of the Sovereign Military Order of

Malta; Walter Brandmüller, president emeritus of the Pontifical Committee for Historical Sciences; and Joachim Meisner, archbishop emeritus of Cologne) to the Holy Father and Cardinal Gerhard Müller, prefect of the Congregation for the Doctrine of the Faith.[29] Less than one year later another letter critical of *Amoris Laetitia*, the "Correctio filialis," was sent to the pope and made public on September 24, 2017.[30]

These oppositions to *Amoris Laetitia* have come from a small number of Catholic aristocrats and intellectuals representing circles already known for their rejection of the teachings of Vatican II and their ideological proximity to traditionalist circles (such as the schismatic group of the Society of St. Pius X and other traditionalist, quasi-schismatic movements within Roman Catholicism). This confirms the periodizing role of the bishops' synods of 2014 and 2015 and of *Amoris Laetitia* as the chronological center of a pontificate consciously facing a new kind of opposition to the papal magisterium in the Catholic Church: those who literally consider themselves more Catholic than the pope.

The second key element of Francis's pontificate, which emerged in the reception of the two synods and *Amoris Laetitia*, is the different reception of papal teachings in different areas of global Catholicism. For example, the debate in the United States on particular issues addressed by the synods ("irregular situations" such as divorced and remarried Catholics and homosexuality) and by chapter VIII of *Amoris Laetitia* has no parallel in other areas of the world. From the very beginning of Francis's pontificate, the militant, neoconservative, and neo-traditionalist factions of American Catholicism felt the need to ensure a hermeneutic of absolute literal continuity with John Paul II and Benedict XVI. In the United States and in other provinces of Anglo-Catholicism in the world there has emerged a new wave

---

[29] See Joshua McElwee, "Four Cardinals Openly Challenge Francis over 'Amoris Laetitia,'" *National Catholic Reporter*, November 14, 2016.

[30] See Joshua McElwee, "Scholars Say Correction of Francis for 'Heresy' Marked by Hypocrisy, Lack of Signatories," *National Catholic Reporter*, September 25, 2017.

of Catholic traditionalism (liturgical and otherwise) that Francis's papacy has not created but has helped reveal.

The synods and *Amoris Laetitia* made clear the differentiated receptions of the pontificate in different areas of the world. The churches whose attention is more focused on *Laudato Si'* than on *Amoris Laetitia* are churches belonging to a different cultural tradition as well as to different latitudes and longitudes on the world map. The relevance of pastoral provisions for divorced and remarried Catholics are not the same in the Christian West (where Christianity used to be the default) as they are in the churches of Asia, where Christians have always been a tiny minority and where climate change and the depletion of natural resources represent more imminent existential threats.

The synodal events and *Amoris Laetitia* represent the periodizing center of Francis's pontificate because they were the culmination of one of its key characteristics as a papacy for a new Catholic Church that needs to reassess how the global dimension affects its understanding of the theological and magisterial tradition (*historical* alignment) and how it influences its diversities on the world map (*geographical* alignment).

Permanent Shifts of Francis's Pontificate

The tensions that have become typical of Francis's pontificate are much more related to his reactions to the doctrinal and political (*latu sensu*) balance of Roman Catholicism and to his defiance of the John Paul II–Benedict XVI paradigm than they are to *Amoris Laetitia* alone.

In terms of its place in history, Pope Francis's pontificate is likely to take on a role similar to John XXIII's in contemporary church history, for three reasons.

The first is the link between the emphasis on the poor church and on the personal embodiment of this ecclesiology. The focus on the "poor church, church for the poor" expressed by Pope Francis a few hours after his election comes from Vatican II and from its visionary pope, John XXIII, who in his life always cherished (without ever romanticizing it) the humble social conditions of his family as an integral part of his spiritual life and as a gift. The extraordinary character of John XXIII (Angelo Roncalli) is shown by the fact that he opened the process for the redefinition of the papacy not through a plan or a project, but thanks to the "confluence in him of papal office, personal sanctity, and prophesy—a confluence that is exceptional in church history."[31] The second reason is that both Roncalli and Bergoglio brought with them to the Vatican an idea of a church that would be more global and more historical than it was before their election, and they connected this to the signature moments in their pontificates: Vatican II and the synodal experience, respectively. Similar to John XXIII's conciliar aspirations, Francis had confidence in a collegial and synodal church that could bring in a new consciousness of the role of the church in the global world. Collegiality and synodality are not so much effective church-management strategies as they are ways to make the gospel message heard in today's world.

The third reason is Francis's confidence in the ability of the gospel to run the church, sometimes in defiance of the church's normative dimension. Canon law, the catechism, and the Catholic tradition are read in light of an understanding of the whole Catholic theological and magisterial tradition that came from Vatican II. In Francis, *ressourcement* is not just a renewed attention to the sources of ancient and medieval Christianity but also to the gospel of Jesus Christ. This has critical consequences for his use and understanding of the normative dimension of the church. This move must be viewed together with Francis's meta-doctrinal shift, the primacy of pastorality, which was also the most important theological shift of Vatican II: "The pastorality that marks Vatican II can be defined as the art of giving men and women access to the one source of the Gospel message."[32]

For these three reasons, and many others, Francis's pontificate can be seen as transitional only in the sense that it is about the shift from a balance that was assumed to be definitive to a different—maybe not necessarily new—kind of balance in Catholicism.

---

[31] Giuseppe Alberigo, *Papa Giovanni XXIII 1881–1963* (Bologna: EDB, 2000), 9.

[32] Theobald, *Accéder à la source*, 697. See also Christoph Theobald, *"Dans les traces . . ." de la constitution 'Dei Verbum' du Concile Vatican II. Bible, théologie, et pratiques de lecture* (Paris: Cerf, 2009).

1

Pope Francis, Global Catholic

Papacy and Catholicism
between Universal and Global

The papacy is one of the most fascinating leadership roles in our world, in part because it is probably the longest-serving (or surely one of the most ancient) such roles in history. It is also a leadership role marked by a claim that is *universal*, that is, conceptually close but not identical to *imperial*. This claim is relevant for understanding the history of Catholicism and of the papacy of Francis in this long history, for two reasons in particular.

The first reason is the interesting paradox of the papal ministry; the perception of this particular role is often associated with the idea of immutability. In a church that has seen significant changes, the function of the papacy has in fact remained structurally and institutionally quite similar to what it was in the 1950s, but it has become even more monarchical, more universal, and more visible for all Catholics. This was particularly evident in the transition between Benedict XVI and Francis in 2013. The reality is that the papacy has changed substantially in two thousand years of history—if we are willing to accept the idea that some leadership role like the papacy has always existed since the Christian community in the city of Rome had its first leader. And the papacy has changed some in these last fifty or so years, but these changes cannot be perceived adequately from a strictly juridical and institutional point of view.[1]

The second reason has to do with the nature of these changes in relation to the political roots of the papacy. For centuries the papacy has continued to rely on its assets—both material-tangible and immaterial, in the social, political, and cultural imaginary of the Western world—as the successor of the Roman Empire. One way to interpret the history of the papacy is as a long, slow detachment, first from the imperial legacy of the Roman Empire (between the fifth and seventh centuries), then from the Holy Roman Empire (between the Gregorian revolution of the eleventh century and the early modern period), and finally from European Christendom in general (between the Reformation in the sixteenth century and the French Revolution, which opened to the "long nineteenth century"). In a sense the universal claim of the papacy—the spiritual sovereignty of the bishop of Rome over the church spread all around the world—has always been mediated through his relationship with the various political forms taken by European Christianity since the beginning of the fourth-century imperial church of Constantine and Theodosius.

The Second Vatican Council, called by John XXIII in 1959 and celebrated between 1962 and 1965, summed up the historical consequences of the long history of estrangement between the Catholic Church and the political embodiment of Christianity in an empire or in a precise geographical part of the world. Most important, the council read that history in light of a new theology that aimed at re-centering Catholicism around Jesus Christ. The entire tradition, including the theological-political tradition of European Christendom, was thus read in light of the message of Jesus Christ.[2] This is clear not only in the pastoral constitution

---

[1] See Massimo Faggioli, "The Running of a Multicultural World Church in Global Times," in *Envisioning Futures for the Catholic Church*, ed. Staf Hellemans and Peter Jonkers (Washington, DC: Council for Research in Values and Philosophy, 2018), 281–300.

[2] See Giuseppe Alberigo, ed., *History of Vatican II*, 5 vols., English version edited by Joseph A. Komonchak (Maryknoll, NY: Orbis Books, 1995–2006); John W. O'Malley, *What Happened at Vatican II* (Cambridge, MA: Belknap Press of Harvard University Press, 2008); and *Vatican II: The Complete History*, ed. Alberto Melloni (Mahwah, NJ: Paulist Press, 2015).

of Vatican II, *Gaudium et Spes*, the last document approved by the council on December 7, 1965, but also from the very first acts of Vatican II, beginning with the preparation period: the decision of John XXIII in June 1960 to create a Secretariat for Christian Unity in Rome; the opening speech of John XXIII, *Gaudet Mater Ecclesia*, on October 11, 1962, which contained his rebuttal against nostalgia for the past;[3] and the *Message to Humanity*, approved by the council fathers on October 20, 1962:

> It is far from true that because we cling to Christ we are diverted from earthly duties and toils. On the contrary, faith, hope, and the love of Christ impel us to serve our brothers, thereby, patterning ourselves after the example of the Divine Teacher, who "came not to be served but to serve" (Mt. 20:28). Hence, the Church too was not born to dominate but to serve.[4]

Between the nineteenth and twentieth centuries the Catholic Church liberated itself—with the providential (if, at the time, loathed) contribution of the Italian nationalist movement—from the burden of governing a state in the heart of Italy.[5] That gave Catholicism a clearer view of its call to look at the world with a more prophetic voice without totally abandoning all its tools for listening to the world, tools developed in the long history of a church where the papal ministry was political as well as religious:

- a centripetal institutional praxis that collects in Rome the information coming from the peripheries;
- the special position of the Catholic Church in the political and cultural landscape of all countries, including those with

---

[3] See John XXIII, *Gaudet Mater Ecclesia*, October 11, 1962, in *The Documents of Vatican II*, ed. Walter M. Abbott, SJ (New York: America Press, 1966), 712.

[4] Vatican II, "Message to Humanity," in Abbott, *The Documents of Vatican II*, 4–5.

[5] See Paolo Prodi, *The Papal Prince: One Body and Two Souls: The Papal Monarchy in Early Modern Europe*, trans. Susan Haskins (Cambridge: Cambridge University Press, 1987), original in Italian, *Il sovrano pontefice. Un corpo e due anime: la monarchia papale nella prima età moderna* (Bologna: Il Mulino, 1982).

which the Catholic Church does not have a concordat and where Catholics are a small minority;

- the activity of papal diplomacy on a wide range of issues; and
- the presence of the Holy See in international and intergovernmental organizations, beginning with the United Nations.

It is not an overstatement to say that the Catholic Church can see the world in a different way than any other individual church or federation of churches or religious tradition. Within Catholicism, the papacy is the first, most important, particularly sensitive receptor of the global world.

Catholicism and Western Identity: From Pius XII to Benedict XVI

During the twentieth century Catholicism realized the need to leave behind some of the theological and institutional legacy of European Christendom, a legacy that the two world wars had tested in many ways.

The pope who had to take stock of the theological crisis made clear by the two world wars and the rise of authoritarian and totalitarian regimes in Europe was Pius XII (1939–58). The papacy of Pius XII was becoming a global papacy, and the Jubilee of 1950 was his way of calling for a reconciliation after the two world wars, and in the context of the Cold War.[6] But his papacy was also marked by his criticism of the new theology, as seen in his 1950 encyclical, *Humani Generis*. This document was part of a larger reaction against the engagement with modernity by Catholic theology at the beginning of the decolonization of the global world as well as of the cultural decolonization of Roman Catholicism from the dominance of Italian and Southern European culture. The confrontation with secularism and atheistic

---

[6] See Robert A. Ventresca, *Soldier of Christ: The Life of Pope Pius XII* (Cambridge, MA: Harvard University Press, 2013); and Michael Phayer, *Pius XII, the Holocaust, and the Cold War* (Bloomington: Indiana University Press, 2007).

ideologies was framed also in political terms: "Prisoner of his still very traditional ecclesiology, he exercised [his authority] more in the narrow, canonical sense of the defense of the rights of the institution and its members than in the broad sense, 'prophetic,' of the moral conscience of humanity. This is undoubtedly one of the limits of his pontificate."[7] During Vatican II and the post–Vatican II period, the pontificate of Paul VI (1963–78) had to grapple with the conciliar and postconciliar dimensions of the Catholic Church in a new global dimension. Paul VI steered Vatican II toward its conclusion and defended its achievements, beginning with its call for liturgical reform. The institutional reforms in the Vatican (of the Roman Curia in the apostolic constitution *Regimini Ecclesiae Universae* of 1967) centralized church government around the pope,[8] and the papacy also became more globally engaged through international trips, advocacy for peace and development (as seen in the encyclical *Populorum Progressio* of 1967), and ecumenical meetings (with the patriarch of Constantinople, Athenagoras, in Jerusalem in January 1964).[9] At the same time, Paul VI was unwilling to break with previous tradition (as seen in his 1968 encyclical *Humanae Vitae*): "The great concern of Paul VI throughout Vatican II was to inscribe the reforming work of the council in continuity with the teachings of the preceding councils, especially those of Vatican Council I on papal primacy and infallibility."[10] His theological culture thus remained very

---

[7] Philippe Chenaux, *Pie XII: Diplomate et Pasteur* (Paris: Cerf, 2003), 416.

[8] See Andrea Riccardi, *Il potere del papa da Pio XII a Giovanni Paolo II* (Rome: Laterza, 1993); idem, "L'evoluzione della Segreteria di Stato dopo il 1870," in *Les Secretaires d'Etat du Saint-Siege, XIX–XX siècles, Melanges de l'École Française de Rome* 116, no. 1 (2004), 33–44; and Joël-Benoît D'Onorio, "Paul VI et le gouvernement centrale de l'église (1968–1978)," in *Paul VI et la modernité dans l'église* (Rome: École Française de Rome, 1984), 615–45.

[9] See Andrea Riccardi, *Manifesto al mondo. Paolo VI all'ONU* (Milan: Jaca Book, 2015).

[10] Philippe Chenaux, *Paul VI. Le souverain éclairé* (Paris: Cerf, 2015), 314. See also Fulvio De Giorgi, *Paolo VI. Il papa del moderno* (Brescia: Morcelliana, 2015); and Jörg Ernesti, *Paul VI. Der vergessene Papst* (Freiburg i.Br.: Herder, 2012).

European and Italian, and his focus on Europe was not limited to a lack of contacts with the Americas.

A different way of defending Vatican II came to the papacy with the election in 1978 of John Paul II, Karol Wojtyla from then-Communist-ruled Poland, the first non-Italian pope since the Dutch Adrian VI (reigned 1522–23). John Paul II strengthened the traditional doctrine on priestly celibacy, was opposed to the ordination of women, and was especially against Latin American liberation theology. On the other hand, John Paul II was clearly innovative with regard to some traditional issues because of his interpretation of Vatican II; he had a much stronger emphasis on the role of lay people in the church, on the role of families in the church, and on the theology of love and sexuality in marriage.

John Paul II also accelerated the Catholic Church's engagement with the ecumenical movement. From his visit to Mainz in Germany in 1980, to the 1995 encyclical *Ut Unum Sint*, to the *Joint Declaration on Justification* with the Lutheran World Federation in 1999, the ecumenical engagement of the Catholic Church was built by John Paul II on the foundations of Vatican II, but also on a much stronger papacy in a more interconnected world. The role of the papacy was evident also in interreligious dialogue, which was ever more important in the world of the "comeback of God" in international affairs. From John Paul II's meeting with Muslim youth in Casablanca (Morocco) in 1985, to the first visit of a pope to the synagogue of Rome in 1986, to the visit to Syria in 2001, the Catholic Church of John Paul II became a key international advocate for dialogue and peace among religions and for religious liberty. He saw the need for this before many others, as evidenced by his idea (widely criticized in the Vatican at the time) of gathering in Assisi in 1986 the first interreligious meeting of prayer for peace. In this sense the globalism of John Paul II was a counterbalance against both neoliberal and neoconservative American culture.[11]

---

[11] See Andrea Riccardi, *Giovanni Paolo II. La biografia* (Cinisello Balsamo: San Paolo, 2011), for an interpretation quite different from the one offered by George Weigel, especially in *Witness to Hope: The Biography of Pope John Paul II* (New York: Harper, 2005).

The terrorist attacks of 9/11 and the rise of international terrorism had an impact on the Catholic Church's reception of Vatican II as well as on its role on the global stage. On one hand, the necessity and prophetical nature of the teachings of Vatican II and of the postconciliar papacy on ecumenism, religious liberty, freedom of conscience, and interreligious dialogue became even clearer. On the other hand, the deep crisis within Islam that caused the rise of terrorism gave some in the church reason to criticize Vatican II for being too naively prone to dialogue in a world that they perceived took advantage of the new, more open stance of the Catholic Church. In this sense the election of Benedict XVI in 2005 was a continuation of some of the theological trajectories of John Paul II that were related to Vatican II, but with a much more cautious position about ecumenism, interreligious dialogue, and dialogue with the modern world.

One example of this increased caution may be found in the Regensburg lecture of September 12, 2006; although it was not directly focused on conciliar hermeneutics, it revealed Benedict XVI's parameters for the relationship of Christianity and the Catholic Church to its Greek and European heritage. It became more and more obvious that the church of Benedict XVI was undergoing a "re-Europeanization" and distancing itself somewhat from the idea of Vatican II as a council of the global Catholic Church, especially of the non-European churches. In the most important of all of Benedict XVI's statements on Vatican II, his speech of December 22, 2005, on the two hermeneutics of the council, he warned that a hermeneutic of "discontinuity and rupture" with the tradition had to be countered with a hermeneutic of "continuity and reform." This was clearly informed by his interpretation of the consequences of the decentralized reception of Vatican II in the new global Catholic Church.[12]

"From the Ends of the Earth": John XXIII and Francis

The pontificate of Pope Francis represents a continuation and an evolution of the globalization of the papacy started in the

---

[12] See Massimo Faggioli, *A Council for the Global Church: Receiving Vatican II in History* (Minneapolis: Fortress Press, 2015), esp. 13–35.

nineteenth century.[13] There are many continuities with and changes from his predecessors. But there are striking similarities between Angelo Giuseppe Roncalli—John XXIII (pope from 1958 to 1963)[14]—and Jorge Mario Bergoglio—Francis (elected in 2013).[15] An analysis and comparison of John XXIII and Francis that focuses on their commonalities and differences can tell us something about the evolution of the papacy and about Francis's papacy in particular.

A Pope from the Countryside and a Pope from the Capital City

John XXIII and Francis's emphasis on the poor reflects (in different ways) the fact that both came from families of limited financial means. Both families were from Northern Italy: Lombardia for Roncalli; Piedmont for Bergoglio's father, Mario; and Genoa for his mother, Regina Maria Sivori.

Angelo Giuseppe Roncalli was born on November 25, 1881, in a village called Sotto il Monte (literally, "under the mountain"), ten miles from Bergamo, thirty-five miles northeast of Milan. He was the fourth of thirteen children; his extended family comprised more than thirty members. The Roncalli family lived

---

[13] See John W. O'Malley, *Vatican I: The Council and the Making of the Ultramontane Church* (Cambridge, MA: Harvard University Press, 2018).

[14] For Angelo Giuseppe Roncalli, see Massimo Faggioli, *John XXIII: The Medicine of Mercy* (Collegeville, MN: Liturgical Press, 2014), a work based on Roncalli's diaries in *Edizione nazionale dei diari di Angelo Giuseppe Roncalli–Giovanni XXIII*, published by the Fondazione per le scienze religiose di Bologna in ten volumes (Bologna, 2003–2008); Alberto Melloni, *Papa Giovanni. Un cristiano e il suo concilio* (Turin: Einaudi, 2009); and Enrico Galavotti, *Processo a papa Giovanni. La causa di canonizzazione di A. G. Roncalli 1965–2000* (Bologna: Il Mulino, 2005).

[15] For Jorge Mario Bergoglio, Pope Francis, see Elisabetta Piquè, *Pope Francis: Life and Revolution: A Biography of Jorge Bergoglio* (Chicago: Loyola Press, 2014), original in Spanish (2013); Austen Ivereigh, *The Great Reformer: Francis and the Making of a Radical Pope* (New York: Holt, 2014); and Paul Vallely, *Pope Francis: Untying the Knots. The Struggle for the Soul of Catholicism,* 2nd ed. (New York: Bloomsbury, 2015; first edition 2013).

a very frugal life, sometimes close to poverty, as was typical of peasants working the land owned by somebody else. In their case the land was owned by the rich Morlani family from Bergamo. Angelo's father was a *mezzadro*, a sharecropper. Jorge Mario Bergoglio was born on December 17, 1936, in Buenos Aires, Argentina. His family had limited means but was closer to the lower middle class than to poor peasants. The major difference between Roncalli and Bergoglio is in terms of existential geography: a peasant family in the countryside versus a family living in the city, something that is evident in the urban and inner-city social imaginary of Pope Francis. Francis is the first pope in the history of the modern papacy who was born in a megalopolis and lived most of his life in an urban environment.

Francis's worldview was shaped by the cosmopolitan character of a pastor born in an immigrant city like Buenos Aires, who never enjoyed traveling,[16] but whose intellectual and spiritual geography was enlarged by the contact with a culture that asserted the centrality of Latin America and the displacement of other coordinates, a correction of the envisioned European model of the relationship between the center and the periphery.[17] John XXIII's view of the world was marked by his international experiences as a bishop's secretary, a Vatican official, and a papal diplomat. There were also significant differences in the lifestyles of the two future popes. Roncalli's young life was much more constraining; seminary life in Italy was very strict about games, the use of local dialect, and sport. Bergoglio had a more "common" life; he worked as a chemist, and had a passion for music, dance, and soccer.[18]

---

[16] See Sergio Rubin and Francesca Ambrogetti, *El Jesuita. Conversaciones con el cardenal Jorge Bergoglio, SJ* (Buenos Aires: Vergara, Grupo Zeta, 2010).

[17] See Massimo Borghesi, *The Mind of Pope Francis: Jorge Mario Bergoglio's Intellectual Journey*, trans. Barry Hudock (Collegeville, MN: Liturgical Press, 2018), 19–55, original in Italian (Milan: Jaca Book, 2017).

[18] This aspect has only a limited part in the recent biopic of Francis, the movie *Chiamatemi Francesco (Call Me Francis)*, directed by Daniele Luchetti (Italy-Argentina, 2015). The biopic's focus is on Bergoglio's actions during the military regime and the Dirty War while a provincial of the Jesuits in Argentina.

A lot had changed in the world between the early 1900s in Roncalli's life and the 1950s for Bergoglio, and there are many differences between Roncalli's Italy and Bergoglio's Argentina. But both men had an interesting issue with vacations. Young Roncalli in his spiritual diary blamed "maledette vacanze!" (damned holidays) for his inability to remain focused on his devotional and spiritual practices (but when he became a cleric and a diplomat, he took long vacations traveling back to Italy).[19] Bergoglio as pope has taken no vacation, never spent time in the papal summer residence in Castel Gandolfo, and even turned it—during the summer of 2015—into a museum.

Roncalli had a clerical formation from a very young age, whereas Bergoglio explored more as a youth. For example, Roncalli never mentioned thinking about a girl as a distraction from the calling to the priesthood. Bergoglio had to work with women who were his superiors or counterparts before joining the Jesuits, as a provincial of the Jesuits, and as a bishop. But Bergoglio also worked with women in difficult personal and social situations.[20] The social and political situation of the early life of the two popes was not radically different. Roncalli was born in a very young, united Italy run by secularist and anticlerical politicians in a still very Catholic country that would soon become polarized between different political ideologies. Bergoglio came of age in an Argentina polarized between an atheistic and anticlerical left and Peronism (an authoritarian and nationalist ideology that brought together the army, the unions, and the church), which Bergoglio got in touch with while in school: "He always had a natural affinity with the cultural and political tradition represented by Peronism."[21]

---

[19] Pope John XXIII, *Journal of a Soul*, trans. Dorothy White (London: Chapman, 1965); in Italian see Angelo Giuseppe Roncalli—Giovanni XXIII, *Il Giornale dell'Anima: Soliloqui, note e diari spirituali*, ed. Alberto Melloni (Bologna: Istituto per le scienze religiose, Fondazione per le scienze religiose Giovanni XXIII, 2003), 21–24 (spiritual notes for the year 1895).

[20] On Bergoglio's work to rescue trafficked women sold into prostitution, see Ivereigh, *The Great Reformer*, 328–32.

[21] Ibid., 30.

Both countries were overwhelmingly Catholic, shaped by Christianity in the form of Christendom; that is, the church had a strong hand in social and political life, but without a political party of Catholics. This changed for Roncalli at the end of World War II, when post-Fascist Italy started being governed by a party of Italian Catholics, Democrazia Cristiana. The party endured until the early 1990s, when it was dissolved in the aftermath of a series of scandals.

For both Roncalli and Bergoglio, the church was a church of devotions, where traditional Catholicism struggled to update itself. For the young priest Roncalli there was the anti-modernist purge launched by Pius X in 1907; for the young Jesuit Bergoglio in the early 1970s the theology of liberation represented a challenge to the cultural unity of a clergy formed before Vatican II. Both popes distanced themselves from these theological streams considered dangerous by the church hierarchy when they were young, but as popes they both reclaimed something of these allegedly dangerous theologies that became key elements for understanding their pontificates (history and tradition for John XXIII; the poor for Francis). There are some ambiguities or, better, ambivalences in how both young clerics dealt with key theological issues of their time. For Roncalli, as nuncio in Paris (1945–53), it was the issue of the worker-priests in France; for Bergoglio as provincial, it was the obedience of the Jesuit priests living in the *villas miserias* (slums).

Difficult Careers of Two Young Clerics

Important differences between the future pope who called Vatican II and the future first pope ordained after Vatican II can be observed in their studies and in their early careers. Roncalli studied in the seminary of his hometown, Bergamo, where he emerged as a very gifted student and then moved to Rome, where he studied at one of the most prestigious theological schools, the Seminario dell'Apollinare (later, the Pontificio Seminario Romano Maggiore). Roncalli studied history by reading very advanced scholars for the time (especially French church historian Louis Duchesne) in an ecclesial environment that was very complicated and dangerous for historians. Those were the years of anti-modernism, and one of his classmates and friends in school was Ernesto Buonaiuti, who was excommunicated in 1925 (and prohibited from teaching also in Italian state universities, thanks to the 1929 Concordat between the church and the Fascist regime). Roncalli was a Milanese or Lombard priest more than a Roman or Vatican priest.[22]

Bergoglio never studied in Rome, and only briefly in Chile (1960) and Spain (1970) and later in Germany for a (failed) doctoral dissertation. His formation was not historical but mostly literary. Interestingly, the Catholic Church in Chile in the early 1960s was one of the most "conciliar" and progressive theological schools (the early proposal of the bishops of Chile for a document on the church was one of the most advanced during the preparation of Vatican II), but it did not seem to have had an impact on the young Bergoglio. His culture was more eclectic and more marked by the political struggles of Argentina (Communism and Peronism) in the 1950s and 1960s. Jesuit spiritual formation is evident also in Roncalli, given the Jesuit culture permeating Italian seminaries during the late nineteenth century.[23] Roncalli's foreign experiences were in Eastern Europe, Turkey, and France, and French was (besides Latin, of course) the language of the young scholar and diplomat. But even before becoming bishop Roncalli had the opportunity to travel north of Italy as secretary of his bishop (to Switzerland, Munich, Salzburg, Krakow, and Budapest). In contrast, Bergoglio's experiences are very Latin American and Spanish; Germany does not seem to have left deep marks in his formation (except for his frequent references to Romano Guardini).[24]

With regard to the United States, for Roncalli those were the very same years—immediately following the condemnation of Americanism by Leo XIII in 1899—when Italian Catholicism was looking with curiosity at American Catholicism and

---

[22] See Stefano Trinchese, "A. G. Roncalli e i sospetti di modernismo," in *Il modernismo tra cristianità e secolarizzazione*, ed. Alfondo Botti and Rocco Cerrato (Urbino, Italy: Quattroventi, 2001), 727–70.

[23] See Maurilio Guasco, *Seminari e clero nel Novecento* (Cinisello Balsamo: San Paolo, 1990).

[24] Romano Guardini's influence on Bergoglio is especially visible in the encyclical *Laudato Si'* (May 24, 2015).

at important episcopal figures in the United States like James Gibbons, John Ireland, and John Lancaster Spalding. Roncalli especially studied Spalding, who delivered an important lecture in Rome in the spring of 1900 on education and cultural renewal in the church.[25] Roncalli never visited the United States, but as a young priest dealing with the missionary activity of the church first and as a diplomat later he had contact with American clerics (for example, the future cardinal of New York Francis Spellman).[26] Bergoglio, in contrast, had no contact with the United States and has visited the United States only in September 2015 as pope; the United States became the more sensitive and critical receptor of his pontificate, and the headquarters of the theological-political opposition to Francis coming from circles opposed to the de-Westernization of Catholicism.

One similarity can be found in the ecclesial and political circumstances that influenced the lives of the two young future popes. For Roncalli, it was the anti-modernist purge and the tight but not tension-free relationship between the Catholic Church and the Fascist regime of Mussolini; for Bergoglio, it was the theology of liberation and the internal rifts between the Argentine church and Jesuits, and the military dictatorship. All this is relevant because both had a difficult time dealing with the Roman Curia. Roncalli's career was more seamless than Bergoglio's, but as a young diplomat (especially while at the diplomatic post in Bulgaria and Turkey) he had a very troubled relationship with Rome, in part because of the accusations of lack of dogmatic rigor launched against Bishop Radini Tedeschi when Roncalli was his secretary.[27] Bergoglio's relations with the Jesuit General Curia in Rome were just as complicated, until a few days after his election to the pontificate on March 13, 2013.

---

[25] See Daniela Saresella, *Cattolicesimo italiano e sfida americana* (Brescia: Morcelliana, 2001); and Ornella Confessore, *L'americanismo cattolico in Italia* (Rome: Studium, 1984).

[26] See Angelo Giuseppe Roncalli (John XXIII), *Tener da conto. Agendine di Bulgaria 1925–1934*, vol. 3 in *Edizione nazionale dei diari di Angelo Giuseppe Roncalli—Giovanni XXIII*, ed. Massimo Faggioli (Bologna: Fondazione per le scienze religiose, 2008).

[27] See Faggioli, *John XXIII: The Medicine of Mercy*, 38–39, 47–48, 55–65.

His news-making interview with Antonio Spadaro, SJ, editor of *Civiltà Cattolica,* September 19, 2013, was also a signal to Jesuits all around the world about the end of the legacy of difficult relations between the Society of Jesus and the papacy through this new Jesuit pope.[28] Despite the uncertainties at the time of his election, Francis's relationship with the Jesuits is one of the most typical markers of his pontificate, especially in terms of his efforts to articulate, translate, and root his message about the church as it undergoes its process of globalization.[29]

Spiritual Rebirth and Pastoral Ministry as Bishops

A similar turnaround moment occurred for both men at the beginning of their pastoral ministry as bishops. It is in their ministry as diocesan bishops that we see them flourish and show signs of what their future pontificates would be.

Engaging in pastoral care as a bishop—like his beloved Bishop Charles Borromeo, the most important bishop in post-Tridentine Europe—had been Roncalli's dream.[30] It was a dream he had fulfilled only partially as a bishop-diplomat when he was in Bulgaria, Turkey, and France between 1925 and 1953. Roncalli was appointed patriarch of Venice in 1953, when he was seventy-two, while Bergoglio was appointed an auxiliary bishop in 1992, when he was fifty-five. Venice in the 1950s was a small and quiet city with a prestigious ecclesiastical see compared to a nation's capital and megalopolis with populated slums like Buenos Aires in the 1990s.

For Bergoglio, the appointment to auxiliary bishop was a rescue from an ecclesiastical wilderness and the beginning of what may be called "the born-again pope," in terms of the spiritual and ecclesial rebirth that became visible after his election to the

---

[28] See Antonio Spadaro, SJ, "Intervista a Papa Francesco," *La Civiltà Cattolica,* 3918 (simultaneously published in different languages in sixteen different Jesuit magazines throughout the world, and in English in the Jesuit magazine *America* with the title "A Big Heart Open to God" [September 19, 2013], 449–77).

[29] See Andreas R. Batlogg, *Der Evangelische Papst. Hält Franziskus, was er verspricht?* (Munich: Kösel, 2018), 67–96.

[30] See Roncalli, *Il Giornale dell'Anima,* 412 (May 1953).

papacy.[31] That appointment—thanks to Cardinal Antonio Quar-
racino, a bishop very different from what Bergoglio would turn
out to be in that role—came after a decisive period in which the
authoritarian and loathed Bergoglio changed into the Bergoglio
we know as Pope Francis. The two years of exile in Cordoba[32]
represented a turning point for him, both spiritually and theologically, in terms of leadership style.

Something similar happened to
Roncalli's spirituality but at a much younger age, in Rome, when
Roncalli was in his twenties, and then to Roncalli's ecclesiology
as a young diplomat and bishop in Bulgaria in his forties.

Both men had similar contact with secularized culture and
with socialism and communism. Venice in the 1950s was a
beacon for modern art and also shared a border with Eastern
Europe; in 1956 a few thousand Hungarian refugees fleeing
the Soviet invasion of Hungary came to Venice. When Buenos
Aires was hit by the financial crisis in 2001–2, Bergoglio acted
as *defensor civitatis*, an advocate for the urban poor. In contrast, Roncalli's relations with the poor and with the blue-collar
workers of Venice were much more indirect, mediated through
a much more traditionally ecclesiastical lifestyle. At this point
there were more similarities between Bishop Bergoglio and the
"social" bishop of Bergamo, Giacomo Maria Radini Tedeschi,
whom Roncalli served as a secretary between 1905 and 1914,
than there were between Bergoglio and Roncalli.

Roncalli and Bergoglio also had different relationships with
their respective political environments. In his diaries Roncalli
observes the convulsions of Italy in the twentieth century—
anticlericalism, Fascism and Mussolini, the Second World War,

---

[31] This is the most important shift, according to Paul Vallely (*Pope
Francis*, 2nd ed., 111–25). From a theological point of view there is the
need to investigate more about Bergoglio and the similarities between
the language of Calvin and Ignatius of Loyola, despite the fact that before becoming an archbishop, Bergoglio spoke of Calvin and Luther in
less than flattering terms (see Jorge Mario Bergoglio, *Chi sono i gesuiti*
[Bologna: EMI, 2014; Buenos Aires, 1987]).

[32] In 1990, in response to complaints from his fellow Argentinian
Jesuits about his authoritarian style, Bergoglio's Jesuit superiors in Rome
sent him to Cordoba, a city four hundred miles from Buenos Aires,
where he was separated from his peers and spent a great deal of time
in isolation.

and the birth of democracy—with an attentive eye. He was always careful not to reveal too much and cautioned his family members not to become too involved and not to trust Fascism. In contrast, Bergoglio seems to have been much more of a political animal, eager to tackle political issues that were also social. What they have in common as bishops, cardinals, and popes is the extreme care they have taken to not become politicized by the clericalist factions of their political milieu—and this caution is something the reactionary factions of the church use to accuse them of being compliant with communism.

Roncalli came from a poor family, but he spoke of a church open to *aggiornamento* without talking of the poor in the radical style later shown by Bergoglio. Perhaps this is because Bergoglio's life experiences had put him much more in contact with the poor. It is interesting to note that Bergoglio, a lower-middle-class Catholic, worked much more closely with the poor than Roncalli, a Catholic from a poor family. Roncalli's clerical status elevated him to a level that was, in the first half of the twentieth century in Italy, significantly different from the social status of the poor in Italy. One point of contact between the two popes is found in the Italian public intellectual Pier Paolo Pasolini, who dedicated a poem and his 1964 film *The Gospel according to Matthew* to John XXIII, and whose language and poetic social imaginary with the poor at the center were close to the language of Pope Francis.

Finally, we should note that their ministries of mercy as pope have some common themes as well, especially in such iconic moments as Pope John XXIII's visit to the Roman prisons (not far from the Vatican) on December 26, 1958, and Pope Francis's many visits to prisons during Holy Week in Rome, in Italy, and during his trips abroad.

Elected in End-of-an-Age Conclaves

There are also many similarities between the conclaves of October 1958 and March 2013. The most visible parallel is in the age of the new popes—seventy-six years of age for both. However, the 1958 conclave had eleven ballots, whereas there were just five in 2013.

The conclave that elected Roncalli came after the pontificates of Pius XI, 1922–39, and Pius XII, 1939–58), which were marked by the dramatic showdown between the church and the authoritarian and totalitarian political ideologies that culminated in the Second World War. Internally, the Catholic Church of that period was focused on disciplining theologians and keeping firm control over organizations of lay Catholics and over Catholic politicians. The conclave of 1958 was the end of an era; it was an "open conclave" in the sense that there was no clear frontrunner (unlike the previous conclave of 1939). An important agenda item for many cardinals in the conclave was the restoration of normal functioning in the ecclesiastical bureaucracy by means of the naming of new cardinals for a depleted college; the appointment of a secretary of state (a position never filled by Pius XII after the death of Cardinal Luigi Maglione in 1944); and a gentle reorganization (but *not* a reform) of the Roman Curia. Very few in the electoral college in 1958 were looking for an eventful pontificate.

The conclave of 2013 took place after two different pontificates—those of John Paul II and Benedict XVI—that were nonetheless connected, and not only by a chronological continuity. The previous thirty-five years can be seen as one long pontificate developing under two strong and cooperative personalities, Karol Wojtyla and Joseph Ratzinger. The final period of this long pontificate was marked by a series of scandals: the sex-abuse scandal; the blatant mismanagement of the church bureaucracy; the growing sense of isolation between Rome and the rest of the church; and, especially, an estrangement between the pope and his closest advisers, on one side, and the Roman Curia, on the other. The conclave of 2013 opened with a sense of urgency because of the resignation of Benedict XVI (with open questions about the reasons for his historic decision) and because of the clouds hanging over Catholicism about the recent record of dealing with the sexual misconduct of the clergy. The conclave of 2013 sought a man who would be able to fix the institutional problems without making dramatic decisions affecting the status quo.

In both 1958 (John XXIII) and 2013 (Francis) the conclaves elected a cardinal they thought would meet their expectation for a quiet and short pontificate. As we know, however, the pontificates of John XXIII and Francis differed from the expectations of most of the cardinal electors. The gap between the expectations and the pontificates is even more shocking in the case of Francis, because Cardinal Bergoglio had attended the conclave of 2005. The cardinals voting in 2013 thought they knew the Argentinian cardinal well because they had already considered him for the papacy eight years before, and they did not imagine that after losing to Cardinal Ratzinger in 2005 he would learn so much about the modern papacy by observing and reflecting upon the actions and words of Benedict XVI.

Four Points of Convergence between the Two Pontificates

There are several points of convergence between the ways the pontificates of John XXIII and Francis unfolded. The first point of convergence is their vision of church reform as spiritual reform. Their decision to seek church reform through conciliar means is part of their ecclesiological imagination; they believed in a church open to the Spirit. Roncalli called Vatican II to be a "new Pentecost," while Francis framed the bishops' synods of 2014–15 in terms of discernment. Their plans were mostly connected to a collegial procedure rather than to setting a particular goal before the process had begun, and about changing the paradigm for the interpretation of doctrine more than about change in doctrine.

The second point of convergence is their message of the openness of the church to renewal. This was seen in the emphasis on unity and mercy by John XXIII (in Vatican II), and by the emphasis on the poor and on mercy by Francis (in the synods and the Extraordinary Jubilee of Mercy). For both popes change is about conversion of the church from a predetermined model to a model following Jesus Christ in a recurrent call to the gospel as ultimate reference for the church. For both popes change is about institutional *reform* but also about spiritual and theological *renewal*.

The third point of convergence is the need to deal with a dysfunctional bureaucratic machine in the Vatican and their interpretation of that mandate. Both popes were elected to fix an institutional problem, and they responded to that, but also to much more. John XXIII called the Second Vatican Council, Francis the synodal process of 2014–15 (followed by the Extraordinary

Jubilee of Mercy of 2015–16). The way of reforming the church without focusing only on fixing structural problems arose as a consequence of their shared ecclesiology, which was not focused on the institution.

The fourth point of convergence is a particular geopolitical situation of the Catholic Church. John XXIII inherited a church that was supposed to be firmly on the side of NATO and the anti-Communist alliance at the height of the Cold War. His last encyclical, *Pacem in Terris* (April 11, 1963), liberated the church from this geopolitical and ideological alignment, a shift already somewhat implicit in Vatican II. Francis inherited a post–9/11 Catholicism in which the neoconservative narrative sees the church as part of an ideological and political anti-Muslim alliance. Francis has also disavowed that ideological narrative of Catholicism. In this sense the political pushback against John XXIII's encyclicals *Mater et Magistra* (1961) and *Pacem in Terris* (1963) are analogous to the ideological criticism of the exhortation *Evangelii Gaudium* (2013) and of the encyclical *Laudato Si'* (2015, a preemptive criticism in this particular case).[33]

Engendering and Responding to an Evolving Catholic Church

What do these two pontificates tell us about the evolution of the papacy in modern times? Beyond their similarities and differences, is there a pattern or trajectory? I posit three dimensions.

Conversion Experiences

The first dimension concerns the globalization of Catholicism and its need for a post-institutional and witnessing papacy. Both Roncalli and Bergoglio became pope after a process of spiritual conversion and personal liberation, something Bergoglio talked

---

[33] See, for example, the series of articles published well before the publication of *Laudato Si'* on the webpage of the US-based and Catholic libertarian think tank Acton Institute. See Michael Sean Winters, "Pope Francis vs. Acton Institute," in *National Catholic Reporter*, May 28, 2014.

about openly and Roncalli wrote about in his diary.[34] After years of struggle with his own imperfection in regard to the ideals of sainthood, in his early twenties Roncalli freed himself from the very strict culture of clerical piety and, by the end of his life, embraced a very different ecclesiology from the one he was taught. This intellectual and spiritual conversion was completed when he was in his forties, during his almost twenty years of diplomatic service in Bulgaria and Turkey that opened his eyes to a world that was different from Catholic Italy. In those years he encountered religious pluralism (Eastern Christianity, Judaism, and Islam), the reality of the condition of Catholicism in places far from Rome, and the complexities of the relationships among religion, politics, and nationalism.[35]

There is a confluence of streams in Bergoglio's period of formation that is different from the post–Vatican II experience of a European or North American Catholic. The post–Vatican II period for Latin America has been a time not just of cultural and theological renewal, but also of political revolution.

On top of this, the experience of post–Vatican II for the Catholic Bergoglio must be read together with the experience of post–Vatican II in the Society of Jesus. Bergoglio arrived at his own liberation later in his life, in his fifties, leaving behind the authoritarianism of his period as a provincial of the Jesuits, and he became not a liberation theologian but a "liberated man."[36] Bergoglio is a Jesuit of the post–Vatican II Society of Jesus, in which the shift inaugurated by Vatican II was matched by a change in the leadership of the Society of Jesus toward a *global* religious order, not just in its personnel but in its theological orientation and relation to local cultures.[37] The Jesuits of the post–Vatican II era are no longer the same Jesuits that "desired

---

[34] See Francis in his 2013 interview with Antonio Spadaro, SJ, "A Big Heart Open to God"; and John XXIII in his spiritual diary, *Journal of a Soul*.

[35] See Faggioli, *John XXIII: The Medicine of Mercy*, 53–67.

[36] See Massimo Faggioli, "Jorge Mario Bergoglio—Francesco," in *Enciclopedia dei papi Treccani*, vol. 3 (Rome: Treccani, 2014), 715–21.

[37] See Gianni La Bella, "Pedro Arrupe e la Santa Sede," in *I gesuiti e i papi*, ed. Michela Catto and Claudio Ferlan (Bologna: Il Mulino, 2015), 191–213.

not just the expansion of Catholicism but its uniformity."[38] At the same time, for all the ambivalences of the vision of globalization in the Jesuits in the early modern period, "the Jesuit story of globalization before the triumph of Western hegemony offers this most important lesson: Globalization did not need to happen through the imposition of Western modernization."[39] No wonder that the global, no-borders evangelization project of the Society of Jesus met with deep suspicion, both in the Vatican and in the rising nation-states, beginning in the early modern period shortly after the founding of the order by Ignatius of Loyola.

Bergoglio is a Jesuit following in the footsteps of Jesuits like Teilhard de Chardin, Karl Rahner, Henri de Lubac, Bernard Lonergan, Augustin Bea, and Pedro Arrupe, who developed in rather new ways the relationship between Catholicism and modernity from the point of view of a "Jesuit global ethos."[40] Particularly important is Bergoglio's connection with Arrupe, the "re-founder" of the Society of Jesus who turned the Jesuits away from the previous 150 years of Romanism and papalism and returned the order to the original intuition of a particular and early form of globalization. This Jesuit global ethos is visible also in Francis's attention to the diversity and plurality of languages and forms of communications and embodiments of the Christian experience in the church, and he is not afraid of the accusations of a theological lack of clarity in his teaching.[41] As Ghislain Lafont writes, "The attempts to establish whether one or the other assertion of the magisterium is infallible, definitive, irreformable, etc.—they are a kind of ecclesiastical gymnastics

---

[38] John T. McGreevy, *American Jesuits and the World: How an Embattled Religious Order Made Modern Catholicism Global* (Princeton, NJ: Princeton University Press, 2016), 2.

[39] José Casanova, "The Jesuits through the Prism of Globalization, Globalization through a Jesuit Prism," in *The Jesuits and Globalization: Historical Legacies and Contemporary Challenges*, ed. Thomas Banchoff and José Casanova (Washington, DC: Georgetown University Press, 2016), 278.

[40] McGreevy, *American Jesuits and the World*, 217.

[41] See Severino Dianich, *Magistero in movimento. Il caso papa Francesco* (Bologna: EDB, 2016), 29–33.

that is quite recent in the history of the church."[42] As such, Francis was not troubled by them.

The global citizenship of the Jesuits has been part of the identity of the Society of Jesus from the very beginning, but in a time of nationalization like the nineteenth century, the increased Jesuit global ethos was one of the products of the expulsion and scattering of Jesuits between 1773 and 1814. One could similarly say that the internal exile of Bergoglio from the Jesuits (1990–92)[43] freed him and enabled him to look at the world with rather unique eyes.

This dimension of becoming, through intense spiritual conversion fueled by life experience, what may be called (in a language close to the experience of Protestant evangelical Christianity in the United States) a "born-again pope," matches the theology and ecclesiology of both Roncalli and Bergoglio. They are both successors of academic and intellectual popes (Pius XII for John XXIII and Benedict XVI for Francis), whose approach to reality was much more systematic and dogmatic than historical and experiential. As Roncalli aged and especially as he experienced his episcopal ministry, he opened himself more to the future and looked less to the past. The same is true of Bergoglio. Later in their lives, as bishops of Rome, they vindicated and are vindicating the notion of the possibility of change in the Catholic Church—an idea that had long been seen as a threat. Both retrieve from the past elements of their formation and biography in critical moments in their lives: the history of the councils and church history for Roncalli; the poor and a non-sectarian church (el pueblo) for Bergoglio.

Francis's ecclesiology and spirituality see the world not as an object metaphysically separated from or threatening Christianity, but as the *space* in which *time* opens new processes. This core theological orientation expressed by Francis in *Evangelii Gaudium* (nos. 222–37), where he states that "time is greater than space," "unity prevails over conflict," "realities are more important than ideas," and "the whole is greater than the

---

[42] Ghislain Lafont, *Piccolo saggio sul tempo di papa Francesco* (Bologna: EDB, 2017), 40.

[43] See Ivereigh, *The Great Reformer*, 165–209; Vallely, *Pope Francis*, 111–25; and Piqué, *Francesco. Vita e rivoluzione*, 107–20.

part"[44]—is a genuine and original interpretation of Vatican II. This has consequences not only for understanding the *modus precedendi* of Bergoglio's teaching, but also his approach to the world of this time. His approach is not only pragmatic, but it also perceives the complex relationship between global and local. As he states in *Evangelii Gaudium:*

> An innate tension also exists between globalization and localization. We need to pay attention to the global so as to avoid narrowness and banality. Yet we also need to look to the local, which keeps our feet on the ground. Together, the two prevent us from falling into one of two extremes. In the first, people get caught up in an abstract, globalized universe, falling into step behind everyone else, admiring the glitter of other people's world, gaping and applauding at all the right times. At the other extreme, they turn into a museum of local folklore, a world apart, doomed to doing the same things over and over, and incapable of being challenged by novelty or appreciating the beauty which God bestows beyond their borders. (*EG,* no. 234)

Evolution of a Truly Global Church

The second dimension that is telling of the evolution of the papacy is the relationship the pope sees between the church and the world, but more specifically between the pope and the Curia and Rome, and between the papacy in Rome and the catholicity of the church. Francis here was part of the new, post–Vatican II globalization of the Jesuits and inherited a more global, less Italian Vatican than John XXIII did.

There is also new geopolitics. Both John XXIII and Francis make clear (in different ways) that the papacy is not bound by a North Atlantic and European political and cultural alignment. But there is also a new ecclesiology that overcomes the Rome-centered idea of the church. The papacies of both John XXIII and Francis

---

[44] See Drew Christiansen, SJ, "The Church Encounters the World," *America* (January 6–13, 2014), 20–21.

are global; they break down a paradigm and build a new one, and specifically they "receive"—again in different ways—the end of European Christendom. Pope John XXIII was the first pope of a church that theologically thinks of itself as worldwide and global *de iure* and not only *de facto*; the pontificate of Pope Francis is the first pontificate of a bishop from the world church and not from the Euro-Mediterranean world since the election of Pope Gregory III (731–41), who was of Syrian origin.

A New Kind of Universalism

The third dimension evidencing the papacy's evolution concerns the papal mystique and the church as an institutional and spiritual "empire." In the history of modern Catholicism, from Vatican I onward, the church has seen different types of popes: the kingly pope, Pius IX; the diplomat pope, Pius XII; the pastor pope, John XXIII; the reformer pope, Paul VI; the international-star pope, John Paul II; and the theologian pope, Benedict XVI. The history of the evolution of the pope's image in the last 150 years says a lot more than the theological definitions of the papacy about the relationship among the role of the papacy, the various visions of the church, and the church's role in the world.

John XXIII, the last Vatican diplomat to be elected pope (the last in a series that includes Pius XI and Pius XII, his predecessors, who were eminent diplomats), the pope who called Vatican II, was the first *global* pope to open the church to a global self-understanding. The politics of John XXIII was global not only in terms of its claims—of becoming a church that for the first time advocated universal human rights—but also in terms of representation—representing the Catholic Church in the sense of the *"universal, comprehensive"* character of Catholicism in his experience in Eastern Europe *(geographically)* and in his experience as a church historian *(chronologically)*. Roncalli brought this global understanding of Catholicism to a world and a church divided by the Cold War—a Cold War that from the very beginning of the post–World War II period had made Catholicism an ideological pillar of the so-called Free World in the Western hemisphere. Roncalli addressed the issue of this ideological polarization by a vigorous engagement with the protagonists of the Cold War (especially John F. Kennedy and Nikita Khrushchev in the Cuban missile crisis of October 1962), thus ushering in the beginning of the Vatican *Ostpolitik*, the diplomatic openings of the Holy See toward the Communist governments in Eastern Europe and Russia. But at the same time Roncalli worked at liberating the Catholic Church—both globally and nationally, in Italy—from a preset ideological alliance with anti-communism. The striking fact is not that Pope Francis inherited this legacy of a very geopolitical Catholic Church; this is not a recent invention. The striking fact is that Francis had in common with John XXIII three particular elements: universalism (in the sense of the Latin *universa* and not *universalis*), anti-ideological Catholicism, and a new geopolitics. Francis's universalism is markedly different from that of his predecessors. The papacy of this last global empire called Catholicism has managed to survive as an institution in a social and political context that has seen great change over the last century: from the era of colonial empires to the age of multinational, economic-financial empires; from nationalism to the crisis of legitimacy of the nation-state in the West; from the world dominated by Western powers to a global world increasingly oriented toward the South and East; from the world of the established state religion to the world of religious freedom and, at the same time, of the *"revanche de Dieu"* and of the "clash of civilizations." In the long-term perspective of church history, John XXIII and Francis are two similar moments in a decisive shift from one kind of papacy to another.[45]

Francis does not understand Catholicism as merely allowed to be plural (but only thus far) because its universal claim is a source of globalization (this was the classical thesis). Francis interprets Catholicism as plural also because its universality is a product of the globalization of the modern world.[46] This reveals Francis's freedom with regard to the temptation to dominate the historical narrative with an idea of the nonnecessity of secular world history in order for the church to understand itself. Francis's remarkable liberation from the obsession of Catholic

---

[45] See Massimo Faggioli, *Pope Francis: Tradition in Transition* (New York: Paulist Press, 2015), 21–28.

[46] See Stefan Nacke, *Die Kirche der Weltgesellschaft. Das II. Vatikanische Konzil und die Globalisierung des Katholizismus* (Wiesbaden: VS Verlag, 2010), 40, quoting Karl Rahner, *Das freie Wort in der Kirche. Die Chancen des Christentums* (Einsiedeln: Johannes Verlag, 1953), 57.

cultural and historical self-sufficiency is a fruit of the church's liberation from the European cradle, but it also reflects the awareness that the present moment of globalization dominated by social media means a certain flattening of the difference between local and global, center and periphery.[47] Most of all, Francis's relationship with the global dimension of the contemporary world has to do with his reception of Vatican II and especially of the pastoral constitution *Gaudium et Spes*, with its emphasis on historical consciousness and openness to a new understanding of the world. In *Evangelii Gaudium* Francis quotes from *Gaudium et Spes*, paragraph 36, which focuses on the "autonomy of the earthly affairs," and thus he showed a full and unembarrassed reception of the pastoral constitution of Vatican II:

> The People of God is incarnate in the peoples of the earth, each of which has its own culture. The concept of culture is valuable for grasping the various expressions of the Christian life present in God's people. It has to do with the lifestyle of a given society, the specific way in which its members relate to one another, to other creatures and to God. Understood in this way, culture embraces the totality of a people's life. Each people in the course of its history develop its culture with legitimate autonomy [reference to *Gaudium et Spes*, no. 36]. (*EG*, no. 115)

Challenges to the Globalism of Bergoglio-Francis

One of the most significant challenges to the globalization of the Catholic Church is the new emphasis on identities, especially gender and sexual identities. Francis's understanding of the role of the church is rooted in the political-economic antagonism on behalf of the working people, which is fundamentally different from the understanding of the church as a "cultural warrior" in

---

[47] See Byung-Chul Han, *The Transparency Society* (Stanford, CA: Stanford University Press, 2015), original in German (Berlin: Matthes and Seitz Verlag, 2012).

the moral crusades set in motion by contemporary bio-politics.[48] Aside from the theological reasons for Francis's distance from the Western emphasis on gender and sexual orientation, there are also other factors; for example, his Latin American origin and Jesuit clerical formation put him at somewhat of a disadvantage in comparison to popes like John Paul II and Benedict XVI, who were more familiar with the European and North Atlantic language for the redefinition of traditional gender roles. Still, the spiritual insights of Francis—most notably, his famous "Who am I to judge?" comment regarding homosexuality[49]—have filled a significant cultural gap in the ongoing globalization process of the church. Something similar is visible in Francis's relationship with the issue of the role of women in the church and with feminist theology: his non-ideological candor in his statements about this issue has gained him the patience that would have, and has been, denied to other church leaders and especially to John Paul II and Benedict XVI. The open question now is, how long will the wisdom and spiritual openness of the magisterium allow it to represent magisterial statements that are under stress, given the huge differences in the sensibilities of Catholics in different parts of the world?

Here we see the limits of Francis's ecclesiology of the people. In his 2016 article on the *sensus fidei* in Francis, Jean-François Chiron correctly acknowledged the steps taken by Francis's ecclesiology of synodality, which is rooted in his dynamic use of the *sensus fidei*: "We can therefore consider the use of *sensus fidei* only within the framework of a dynamic. If the *sensus fidei* is a given, we have access to it, or rather it manifests itself only through an institutionalized process of speech. No doubt it is necessary to take distance from a static understanding of *consensus fidelium*, understood only as a unanimity in a given expression of faith."[50] At the same time, Chiron cautiously alluded

---

[48] See Emilce Cuda, *Para Leer a Francisco: Telogia, ética y politica*, preface by Juan Carlos Scannone (Buenos Aires: Manantial, 2016).

[49] See John L. Allen, Jr., "Pope on Homosexuals: 'Who Am I to Judge?'" *National Catholic Reporter* (July 29, 2013).

[50] Jean-François Chiron, "Sensus fidei et vision de l'Église chez le Pape François," *Recherches de Science Religieuses* 104, no. 2 (June 2016), 204.

to the limits of Francis's implementation of synodality. On one hand, Chiron makes clear the necessity for giving institutional dimension to synodality: "the culture of encounter needs to find institutional expression."[51] But on the other hand, Chiron also shows the possible constraints for a truly ecclesial-institutional dimension of synodality in the context of an ecclesiology of the *sensus fidei*, where the *sensus fidei* is seen as expressed in the popular piety alone.

One other area where Francis's spirituality bridges the gap between his roots and the fractures of globalization is in the political situation. As a Catholic who grew up in the political culture of Vatican II, Francis deals with a post–Vatican II world, with a situation that is geopolitically shaped by a set of fault lines and alignments very different from those of the 1960s and 1970s and that domestically has seen the collapse of a sense of unity around nation or class. Notably, Francis's handling of his roots in this political phase of globalization has always been about not making of his native Argentina what John Paul II made of Poland—a model for the entire church.

Finally, the challenge for a post–Vatican II pope like Francis is how to convert the papacy and Catholicism into a counternarrative. The papacy and the church of Vatican II were part of the new world (post–World War II, postcolonial) and its globalization; the church of John Paul II was part of the anti-communist struggle and the victory against communism; and the church of Benedict XVI was part of the post–9/11 reawakening from the hangover of the victory of the Western world over communism and the need to react to the clash of civilizations. Pope Francis's pontificate is not about finding a trending narrative on globalization that the Catholic Church can be part of—quite the opposite, in fact. Francis's global papacy has to deal with a disruption of globalization, and it responds by recapturing the interrupted discourse on Vatican II.

---

[51] Ibid., 199.

2

Francis and the Reception of Vatican II as a Global Council

The conclave of March 2013 took place in a very particular period in the history of the reception of the Second Vatican Council; that is, after the pontificate of Benedict XVI, whose overarching message was clearly about the intention to revisit the Second Vatican Council and its reception and application in the life of the church. In this sense the election of the successor of Benedict XVI was not just the election of the new bishop of Rome, but it was also framed in the context of the debate on Vatican II, a debate in which Benedict XVI had played a very visible role. Indeed, the debate had been prompted by him at the beginning of his pontificate with the famous speech to the Roman Curia on the "two hermeneutics" of December 22, 2005, which was also meant to be the response to the two most important works on Vatican II published in the previous decade: the five-volume *History of Vatican II* directed by the John XXIII Foundation for Religious Studies in Bologna, and the five-volume *Kommentar* on the documents of Vatican II conceived in the department of Catholic theology in Tübingen, where, fifty years earlier, a young Joseph Ratzinger had been hired upon the recommendation of Hans Küng.[1]

---

[1] See *History of Vatican II*, 5 vols., ed. Joseph Komonchak (Maryknoll, NY: Orbis Books, 1995–2006), in Italian, *Storia del concilio*

The pontificate of Benedict XVI represented the culmination of a trend inaugurated before his election. Already toward the end of the pontificate of John Paul II, that is, in the early 2000s, one could see signs of a "policy review" of the Roman Curia about the interpretation and reception of Vatican II—the most consequential being the instructions of the Congregation for Divine Worship, *Liturgiam Authenticam*, of March 28, 2001, which inspired and caused a new trend in the translation of liturgical texts whose fruits are very well known in the English-speaking world, and *Redemptionis Sacramentum*, of April 23, 2004, about liturgical abuses.[2] This trend became even stronger with the election of Benedict XVI. From 2005 onward, Benedict XVI's interpretation of Vatican II was summarized by commentators on the one side as a polarity between "continuity and reform," and on the other between "discontinuity and rupture." This simplistic caricature of the hermeneutical complexity of Vatican II penetrated and shaped the language of the discourse of the Catholic Church on Vatican II, especially at the level of theological studies and seminaries, but also in the theological orientation of bishops and cardinals.

The argument of "continuity with the tradition of the council," which had been presented at the beginning, in Benedict XVI's speech, as an argument not only against liberal-progressive interpretations of Vatican II but also against the Lefebvrian thesis of Vatican II as a rupture with the Catholic tradition, soon showed the real objectives of many interpreters

---

Vaticano II, 5 vols., ed. Giuseppe Alberigo (Bologna: Il Mulino; Leuven: Peeters, 1995–2001); and Peter Hünermann and Bernd Jochen Hilberath, eds., *Herders theologischer Kommentar zum Zweiten Vatikanischen Konzil*, 5 vols. (Freiburg i.B.: Herder, 2004–5). Benedict XVI's implicit but clear criticism of the five-volume *Kommentar* in the speech of December 22, 2005, has been confirmed by Peter Hünermann himself (*"In der Freiheit des Geistes leben": Peter Hünermann im Gespräch*, ed. Margit Eckholt and Regina Heyder [Ostfildern: Matthias-Grünewald, 2010]).

   [2] See Massimo Faggioli, "The Liturgical Reform from 1963 until Today . . . and Beyond," *Toronto Journal of Theology* 32, no. 2 (2016): 201–17.

of that speech of Benedict XVI—and in some instances, of Benedict XVI himself.[3] This is a key element for understanding how Francis's theology interacted with the theological culture identified with the papacy in 2013, and it helps to explain the reception of Francis in the global church today. Pope Francis inaugurated a new phase in the reception of Vatican II, partly due to the disappearance of traditionalist issues from his agenda, which affected his handling of liturgical and other matters.[4] The pontificates of the popes elected since 1939 have all been defined in some measure by the historical-theological debate in relation to the council—from Pius XII's decision not to reconvene Vatican I in 1948–49 to John Paul II, the last pope who had been a member and a key figure of Vatican II and, at the same time, a stabilizer of the council in the post–Vatican II period; to Benedict XVI, one of the most influential theologians at Vatican II.[5] Pope Francis, ordained a

---

[3] See, for example, the lack of clarity in the motu proprio *Summorum Pontificum* (July 7, 2007) about the implications of the liberalization of the pre–Vatican II liturgy for the interpretation of Vatican II. In the letter accompanying the motu proprio, with the same date of July 7, 2007, Benedict XVI writes: "In the first place, there is the fear that the document detracts from the authority of the Second Vatican Council, one of whose essential decisions—the liturgical reform—is being called into question. This fear is unfounded." Moreover, Benedict expressed the wish that "the two Forms of the usage of the Roman Rite can be mutually enriching." On both accounts the reality since the publication of *Summorum Pontificum* has been very different from the one Benedict XVI spoke of in 2007.

[4] See, for example, Francis's speech to Italian liturgists gathered for the 68th National Liturgical Week, August 24, 2017, on the irreversibility and ongoing process of the liturgical reform of Vatican II. About this, see also Cesare Giraudo, SJ, "La riforma liturgica a 50 anni dal Vaticano II. 'Parlare di "riforma della riforma" è un errore,'" *La Civiltà Cattolica*, 3995 (December 10, 2016): 432–45.

[5] See Enrico Galavotti, "Il Concilio di papa Francesco," in *Il Conclave e papa Francesco. Il primo anno di pontificato*, ed. Alberto Melloni (Rome: Istituto della Enciclopedia Italiana, 2014), 35–69; idem, "Jorge Mario Bergoglio e il concilio Vaticano II: fonte e metodo," *Rivista di Teologia dell'Evangelizzazione* 22, no. 43 (2018): 61–88.

priest in 1969, does not belong in this line of popes involved in Vatican II for biographical reasons. But there is also the specific heritage of the Catholic Church in Latin America and the legacy of Vatican II for Latin American Catholicism throughout these last fifty years.

Clearly the Argentinian Jesuit Bergoglio perceives Vatican II as a matter that should not be reinterpreted or restricted but rather implemented and expanded.[6]

There was also something very visible from the very beginning of his pontificate. In the words addressed to the people in Saint Peter's Square after the election, on the evening of March 13, 2013, Francis presented himself as the "bishop of Rome"; the terms *bishop* and *people,* crucial to Francis's ecclesiology, signified from the beginning an emphasis on the ecclesiology of the local church and on the diocese of Rome as a local church.

Francis has quoted Vatican II less than his predecessors, but his quotations have always been carefully chosen to mark particularly important moments during his pontificate. Remarkably, the first mention of Vatican II during his pontificate was one week after his election, March 20, 2013. During a meeting with the fraternal delegates from other churches and religions, Francis mentioned the Second Vatican Council and, in particular, the declaration *Nostra Aetate* (October 28, 1965) on non-Christian religions.

It is impossible to assess Francis's relationship with Vatican II simply from the number of references to the council and its documents in the texts of his teaching. His modality of reception of Vatican II is a complex mix of the *reception* of the documents of the council and of the *act* of the council.

A Spiritual-Theological Reception

The two ecclesiological constitutions, *Lumen Gentium* and *Gaudium et Spes,* are the most important textual references to Vatican II in Pope Francis's teaching; it can be said that Francis's

---

[6] See Massimo Faggioli, *Pope Francis: Tradition in Transition* (Mahwah, NJ: Paulist Press, 2015).

reception of Vatican II is ecclesiological in the sense of a missionary reform of the church. There is also an ecclesiological intention in the selections of the sources in Francis's teachings: of the 217 endnotes in *Evangelii Gaudium*, there are only seven quotations from documents issued by the Roman Curia (four from the *Compendium of the Social Doctrine of the Church* by the Pontifical Council for Justice and Peace, and three from the Congregation for the Doctrine of the Faith from the instruction *Libertatis Nuntio* about the theology of liberation). There are fifteen quotations from Vatican II and twenty-three quotations from documents of national or continental bishops' conferences.

But Francis's response is, above all, a spiritual-theological reception of Vatican II.[7] We can see that from his reception of *Lumen Gentium*.

Lumen Gentium: *Papal Teaching and the Church*

The conciliar constitution on the church, *Lumen Gentium* (November 21, 1964), plays a special role in the relationship between Francis and Vatican II. Pope Francis's apostolic exhortation *Evangelii Gaudium*, which is akin to a programmatic document for his pontificate, quotes the documents of Vatican II twenty times, and the most quoted is *Lumen Gentium*.

Paragraph 12 of *Lumen Gentium* is particularly significant for Francis. In *Evangelii Gaudium* it is clearly his intent to rephrase the infallibility of the magisterium as based on the infallibility of the people of God:

> In all the baptized, from first to last, the sanctifying power of the Spirit is at work, impelling us to evangelization. The people of God is holy thanks to this anointing, which makes it infallible *in credendo*. This means that it does not err in faith, even though it may not find words to explain that faith. (*EG*, no. 119)

---

[7] For the distinction among *kerygmatic, theological,* and *spiritual* reception of a council, see Alois Grillmeier, "The Reception of Chalcedon in the Roman Catholic Church," *Ecumenical Review* 22 (1970): 383–411.

This passage about the *sensus fidei* is even more remarkable because it is the only passage of the exhortation that talks about infallibility, and it does so in terms of infallibility *in credendo* of the people of God. Francis's choice in favor of an ecclesiology of the people as missionary people is more accentuated in *Evangelii Gaudium* than in Vatican II itself (*LG*, no. 17; see also *Ad Gentes, nos.* 5–6). This is also an ecclesiology that has in mind a practical restructuring of ordained ministry in the church, beginning with the bishops:

> [The bishop] will sometimes go *before his people*, pointing the way and keeping their hope vibrant. At other times, he will simply be *in their midst* with his unassuming and merciful presence. At yet other times, he will have to *walk after them*, helping those who lag behind and—above all—allowing the flock to strike out on new paths. (*EG*, no. 31).

The local level is emphasized not only here in the relations between the bishop and the people, but also in the way *Evangelii Gaudium* operates theologically. The sources of the exhortation—much more abundantly than in previous papal teachings, now coming from documents approved by national and continental bishops' conferences—presuppose a *communio ecclesiae* (the communion of the local churches with Rome) not absorbing totally the *communio ecclesiarum* (the communion of the local churches among themselves).[8]

The connection between reform ecclesiology and local ecclesiology leads in *Evangelii Gaudium* to a paragraph on the reform of the Petrine ministry, which Pope Francis connects to the "conversion of the papacy." Francis admits that little progress has been made since Vatican II and since John Paul II's encyclical on ecumenism *Ut Unum Sint* (1995):

---

[8] This is one of the "building sites" left unfinished by Vatican II: see Hervé Legrand, "Communio ecclesiae, communio ecclesiarum, collegium episcoporum," in *La riforma e le riforme nella chiesa*, ed. Antonio Spadaro and Carlos Maria Galli (Brescia: Queriniana, 2016), 159–88.

Pope John Paul II asked for help in finding "a way of exercising the primacy which, while in no way renouncing what is essential to its mission, is nonetheless open to a new situation" [*Ut Unum Sint* 1995, no. 95]. We have made little progress in this regard. The papacy and the central structures of the universal church also need to hear the call to pastoral conversion. (*EG*, no. 32)

Evangelii Gaudium is not the only major teaching of Francis that draws from Vatican II. The encyclical *Laudato Si'* does not quote *Lumen Gentium* but contains indirectly a reception of the ecumenical ecclesiology of Vatican II, expressed also in *Lumen Gentium*, with its inter-Christian appeal and sources.

It is in the post-synodal exhortation *Amoris Laetitia* (March 19, 2016) that Francis makes progress regarding the reception of the ecclesiology of *Lumen Gentium*. From the very beginning of the exhortation Francis reframes the relationship between the papacy and the teaching of the church:

I would make it clear that not all discussions of doctrinal, moral or pastoral issues need to be settled by interventions of the magisterium. Unity of teaching and practice is certainly necessary in the Church, but this does not preclude various ways of interpreting some aspects of that teaching or drawing certain consequences from it. (*AL*, no. 3)

This is by far the most important ecclesiological development in a papal document issued after the very eventful bishops' synods (2014 and 2015) on family and marriage.

Gaudium et Spes:
Recontextualization of the Catholic Church

The reception of *Gaudium et Spes* in Francis's pontificate presents a remarkable reversal of fortune for the last document of Vatican II, the pastoral constitution, from the pontificate of Benedict XVI, who quoted *Gaudium et Spes*, but often in a critical way.[9] Francis's theological thrust is about the recovery of a Catholic universality that is free from Latin universalism and not about a cultural resistance against modernity and postmodernity. The legacy of *Gaudium et Spes* is evident in paragraphs 222 through 237 of *Evangelii Gaudium*, where we have a condensed summary of the worldview of Vatican II in four axioms: "Time is greater than space"; "unity prevails over conflict"; "realities are more important than ideas"; and "the whole is greater than the part."[10] Francis writes, "Giving priority to time means being concerned about initiating processes rather than possessing spaces" (*EG*, no. 223)—a reception of the new awareness expressed by Vatican II about historicity. Then, "Realities are greater than ideas. This principle has to do with incarnation of the word and its being put into practice" (*EG*, no. 233). This is closest to the core of *Gaudium et Spes*'s existential-ontological thesis: also in the realm of concrete spiritual decisions, the particular and individual element cannot, despite the real validity of general principles, be simply drawn general principles. "Time is greater than space" embodies the shift from a purely metaphysical approach to God's revelation to a more tangible "history of salvation." "Realities are more important than ideas" embodies the shift from the deductive to the inductive method.

Francis's pontificate deals with this shift most specifically in his remarkable description of the church as a polyhedron:

> Here our model is not the sphere, which is no greater than its parts, where every point is equidistant from the centre, and there are no differences between them. Instead, it is the polyhedron, which reflects the convergence of all its

---

[9] See, for Joseph Ratzinger's very critical approach to *Gaudium et Spes*, his introduction, in the series of his complete works, to the first of the two volumes dedicated to Vatican II: "Vorwort," in *Zur Lehre des Zweiten Vatikanischen Konzils. Formulierung—Vermittlung—Deutung* (series Joseph Ratzinger Gesammelte Schriften, Band 7/1) (Freiburg i.B.: Herder, 2012), 5–9, esp. 6–7. See also Carlos Schickendantz, "¿Una transformación metodológica inadvertida? La novedad introducida por *Gaudium et Spes* en los escritos de Joseph Ratzinger," *Teología y Vida* 57, no. 1 (2016): 9–37.

[10] See Drew Christiansen, SJ, "The Church Encounters the World," *America* (January 6–13, 2014), 20–21.

parts, each of which preserves its distinctiveness. Pastoral and political activity alike seek to gather in this polyhedron the best of each. There is a place for the poor and their culture, their aspirations and their potential. Even people who can be considered dubious on account of their errors have something to offer which must not be overlooked. It is the convergence of peoples who, within the universal order, maintain their own individuality; it is the sum total of persons within a society which pursues the common good, which truly has a place for everyone. (*EG*, no. 236)

The universality Francis has in mind means a "big tent" church open to the world and opposed to the temptation to create a smaller, purer church made of smaller communities—with some remarkable consequences for the link, often made by papal magisterium in the post–Vatican II period, between the council and the flourishing of postconciliar lay Catholic movements.[11] But what is especially typical of Francis's reception of Vatican II is not only this anti-elitism, but also the retrieval of the almost forgotten emphasis on the poor and the "preferential option for the poor" that finds its source in Vatican II (*LG*, no. 8; *GS*, no. 1; *AG*, no. 3).

The conciliar ecclesiology of the relationship between the church and the world, rooted in *Gaudium et Spes*, is received in *Evangelii Gaudium*: "Jesus did not tell the apostles to form an exclusive and elite group" (no. 114). Also, the discussion about Christian faith and plurality of cultures demonstrates a full and unembarrassed reception of the pastoral constitution of Vatican II by Pope Francis (no. 115).[12]

---

[11] For more on Francis and the new Catholic movements, see Massimo Faggioli, *The Rising Laity: Ecclesial Movements since Vatican II* (Mahwah, NJ: Paulist Press, 2016), 131–53.

[12] The footnote to *Gaudium et Spes* (no. 36) is an indirect reference to the case of Galileo Galilei when the text talks about the compatibility between faith and science. The reference in the footnote is to Pio Paschini, *Vita e opere di Galileo Galilei*, 2 vols. (Vatican City: Pontificia Accademia delle Scienze, 1964). See Alberto Melloni, "Galileo al Vaticano II. Storia d'una citazione e della sua ombra," *Cristianesimo nella Storia* 3, no. 1 (2010): 131–64.

The encyclical *Laudato Si'* draws from *Gaudium et Spes*, although, typical of Francis, its text is not overloaded with conciliar quotations, which are mostly mediated through the use of postconciliar teaching—especially that of Paul VI and the national and continental bishops' conferences.[13] It is remarkable that all quotations from Vatican II in *Laudato Si'* are from *Gaudium et Spes*.

Of all the major documents issued by Francis, *Gaudium et Spes* plays the most prominent role in the exhortation *Amoris Laetitia*. In *Amoris Laetitia*, Francis quotes *Evangelii Gaudium* (ten times), *Gaudium et Spes* (nineteen times), and John Paul II's exhortation *Familiaris Consortio* of 1981 (twenty-six times). As in his previous documents, in *Amoris Laetitia*, Francis cites often from documents of national bishops' conferences (Spain, Korea, Argentina, Mexico, Colombia, Chile, Australia, CELAM, Italy, and Kenya) and, in this particular case, very often from the catechesis of John Paul II. But *Gaudium et Spes* plays a pivotal role for the exhortation, as it did during the entire synodal process of the bishops' synods of October 2014 and October 2015. *Amoris Laetitia* draws from *Gaudium et Spes* for the paragraphs of the pastoral constitution on family and marriage,[14] but also from *Gaudium et Spes*, no. 22, on "Christ the new Adam" (cf. *AL*, nos. 77–78); *Gaudium et Spes*, no. 16, on conscience; and *Gaudium et Spes*, no. 17, on freedom and human dignity.

Sacrosanctum Concilium: *Liturgy and Ecclesiology*

The reception of the liturgical constitution of Vatican II presents a particular aspect of Francis's overall reception of the council. On the one hand, the liturgical issue in the Catholic Church has been one of the most affected by the pontificate of Francis's predecessor;[15] on the other hand, regarding the liturgical issue, Francis's pontificate has been marked by a reception of the

---

[13] For example, the quotation from Paul VI's encyclical *Populorum Progressio* (1967) in *Laudato Si'*, no. 127.

[14] *GS*, nos. 48–50, in *AL*, nos. 80, 125, 126, 134, 142, 154, 166, 172, 178, 222, 298, and 315.

[15] See Faggioli, "The Liturgical Reform from 1963 until Today . . . and Beyond."

teaching of Vatican II that does not reduce the council to a corpus of texts and at the same time is faithful to its trajectories—in this case, to the path toward liturgical reform introduced by Vatican II. This is one way to read the notable absence of quotations from *Sacrosanctum Concilium* in *Evangelii Gaudium*—a document which contains a long section on the homily.

However, Francis's attention to the liturgical issue and its connections to the ecclesiology of Vatican II are evident in *Evangelii Gaudium*. As Francis notes, liturgy is evangelizing and not part of a power struggle in the church, or a way to express an exclusive ecclesiology, or to use the gospel to ignore the deep solidarity between the church and the world:

> This insidious worldliness is evident in a number of attitudes which appear opposed, yet all have the same pretence of "taking over the space of the Church." In some people we see an ostentatious preoccupation for the liturgy, for doctrine and for the Church's prestige, but without any concern that the Gospel have a real impact on God's faithful people and the concrete needs of the present time. In this way, the life of the Church turns into a museum piece or something which is the property of a select few. (*EG*, no. 95)

In *Laudato Si'* Francis expresses (quoting John Paul II's exhortation *Ecclesia de Eucharestia*, 2003) the link between liturgy and a new church-world relationship, speaking of creation and the Eucharist "as an act of cosmic love" (*LS*, no. 236). Also, in *Amoris Laetitia*, quoting again from the teaching of John Paul II, Francis emphasizes an understanding of the liturgy that connects human love and divine love, thus extending the definition of *liturgical* beyond the boundaries of the liturgical rites of the church: "The procreative meaning of sexuality, the language of the body, and the signs of love shown throughout married life, all become an 'uninterrupted continuity of liturgical language' and 'conjugal life becomes in a certain sense liturgical'" (*AL*, no. 215).

This has been a constant impulse coming from Francis: the visible statements about the liturgical reform of Vatican II—in the direction of a rejection of the plans for a "reform of the liturgical reform" of Vatican II—are substantiated by a much larger body of theology of the liturgy in his pontificate.[16]

Dei Verbum: *Exegetes and Theologians*

Among all the major documents of Vatican II that need to be examined to understand Francis's reception of the council, the *Dogmatic Constitution on Revelation (Dei Verbum)* offers a particular comparison with his predecessor, Benedict XVI, for whom *Dei Verbum* was probably the keystone of the conciliar teaching.[17] Francis's theological profile is not that of a biblical scholar. But certainly his preaching is in line with the conciliar re-centering on the gospel of Jesus Christ as the "generative grammar" of Catholic theology and magisterium.[18] "Through this revelation, therefore, the invisible God (see Col 1:15, 1 Tim 1:17)

---

[16] Pope Francis, *Address to the Participants of the 68th National Liturgical Week in Italy*, August 24, 2017: "There is still work to be done in this direction, in particular by rediscovering the reasons for the decisions taken with regard to the liturgical reform, by overcoming unfounded and superficial readings, a partial reception, and practices that disfigure it. It is not a matter of rethinking the reform by reviewing the choices in its regard, but of knowing better the underlying reasons, through historical documentation, as well as of internalizing its inspirational principles and of observing the discipline that governs it. After this magisterium, after this long journey, we can affirm with certainty and with magisterial authority that the liturgical reform is irreversible." See also "Holy See Press Office Communiqué: Some Clarifications on the Celebration of Mass, 11.07.2016," which disavowed the statement by Cardinal Robert Sarah (prefect of the Congregation for the Divine Worship) and the agenda of the "reform of the liturgical reform" (an expression that the Holy See statement says "may at times give rise to error"), which the cardinal recommended to the clergy in a public lecture in London a few days before.

[17] See the reliable and very fascinating commentary on *Dei Verbum* by Joseph Ratzinger, in *Commentary on the Documents of Vatican II*, vol. 3, trans. and ed. Herbert Vorgrimler (New York: Herder and Herder, 1968).

[18] On the "generative grammar" of Vatican II, see Christoph Theobald, *Accéder à la source*, vol. 1 in *La réception du concile Vatican II* (Paris: Cerf, 2009), 894–900.

out of the abundance of His love speaks to men as friends" (*DV*, no. 2). This passage represents Francis's new incarnation of the papacy as a way to be the church not based on the gospel or about the gospel, but the church *of* the gospel. In the famous passages "time is greater than space" and "realities are greater than ideas" (*EG*, nos. 222, 233), there is an indirect but unquestionable reception of the theological insight of *Dei Verbum*, no. 8, about the relationship between human experience and God's revelation.[19]

A Generative Reception

The marker of Pope Francis's reception of Vatican II is not a textual one but what we might call a generative reception of the council. In his pontificate the legacy of the council lives not through quotations from the final documents but in a reception of various conciliar sources and in various ways.

The Key Role of John XXIII's Gaudet Mater Ecclesia

The first way Francis demonstrates his generative reception of the council is through the use of the texts of Vatican II that do not belong to the formal corpus of the final documents of the council. The most important example of this is found in *Evangelii Gaudium*, where he discusses the relationship between the deposit of faith and ways to express it. Pope Francis quotes from John XXIII's opening speech of the council delivered on October 11, 1962, *Gaudet Mater Ecclesia*—a key (and not at all obvious) source from the history of Vatican II from a hermeneutical point of view.[20] Francis writes:

---

[19] See Severino Dianich, *Magistero in movimento. Il caso papa Francesco* (Bologna: EDB, 2016), 63–64.

[20] See Giuseppe Alberigo, "Criteri ermeneutici per una storia del Vaticano II," in Giuseppe Alberigo, *Transizione epocale: Studi sul Concilio Vaticano II* (Bologna: Il Mulino, 2009), 29–45. On Francis and John XXIII's *Gaudet Mater Ecclesia*, see Ormond Rush, *The Vision of Vatican II: Its Fundamental Principles* (Collegeville, MN: Liturgical Press, 2019), 536–39.

At the same time, today's vast and rapid cultural changes demand that we constantly seek ways of expressing unchanging truths in a language which brings out their abiding newness. "The deposit of the faith is one thing. . . . The way it is expressed is another" [*Gaudet Mater Ecclesia*]. There are times when the faithful, in listening to completely orthodox language, take away something alien to the authentic Gospel of Jesus Christ, because that language is alien to their own way of speaking to and understanding one another. With the holy intent of communicating the truth about God and humanity, we sometimes give them a false god or a human ideal which is not really Christian. In this way, we hold fast to a formulation while failing to convey its substance. This is the greatest danger. Let us never forget that "the expression of truth can take different forms. The renewal of these forms of expression becomes necessary for the sake of transmitting to the people of today the Gospel message in its unchanging meaning" [*Ut Unum Sint*, no. 19]. (*EG*, no. 41)

The other important quotation from *Gaudet Mater Ecclesia* is in *Evangelii Gaudium* about the challenges to evangelization and the lack of hope that is typical of our times:

The joy of the Gospel is such that it cannot be taken away from us by anyone or anything (cf. *Jn* 16:22). The evils of our world—and those of the church—must not be excuses for diminishing our commitment and our fervor. Let us look upon them as challenges which can help us to grow. With the eyes of faith, we can see the light which the Holy Spirit always radiates in the midst of darkness, never forgetting that "where sin increased, grace has abounded all the more" (*Rom* 5:20). Our faith is challenged to discern how wine can come from water and how wheat can grow in the midst of weeds. Fifty years after the Second Vatican Council, we are distressed by the troubles of our age and far from naive optimism; yet the fact that we are more realistic must not mean that we are any less trusting in the Spirit or less generous. In this sense, we can once again listen to the words of Blessed John XXIII on the memorable day of 11 October 1962: "At times we have to listen, much to our regret, to the voices of people who, though burning with zeal, lack a sense of discretion and measure. In this modern age they can see nothing but prevarication and ruin. . . . We feel that we must disagree with those prophets of doom who are always forecasting disaster, as though the end of the world were at hand. In our times, divine Providence is leading us to a new order of human relations which, by human effort and even beyond all expectations, are directed to the fulfillment of God's superior and inscrutable designs, in which everything, even human setbacks, leads to the greater good of the Church." (*EG*, no. 84)

In this section of *Evangelii Gaudium*, with the quotations from *Gaudet Mater Ecclesia*, Pope Francis is reenacting Pope John XXIII's reorientation of the church's message, thus showing many parallels between the church at the end of Pius XII's pontificate and at the beginning of his own.[21] Like John XXIII, the election of Francis happened in difficult times for the church, not only because of the external circumstances, but also because of the unstated but clear sense of exhaustion of a given theological-cultural paradigm and the need to reframe and rephrase the message of the church in a new paradigm. It is no surprise, then, that the resistance and fear of change met by John XXIII at the time of the council were similar to the reception of Pope Francis in some quarters of the Catholic Church today. The bull of indiction of the Extraordinary Jubilee of Mercy (*Misericordiae Vultus*, April 11, 2015) quotes again from John XXIII's *Gaudet Mater Ecclesia*. Francis writes:

I have chosen the date of 8 December because of its rich meaning in the recent history of the Church. In fact, I will open the Holy Door on the fiftieth anniversary of

---

[21] For the impact of John XXIII's *Gaudet Mater Ecclesia* on Vatican II, see John W. O'Malley, *What Happened at Vatican II* (Cambridge MA: Belknap Press of Harvard University Press, 2008), 93–96; Andrea Riccardi, "The Tumultuous Opening Days of the Council," in *History of Vatican II*, vol. 2, ed. Giuseppe Alberigo and Joseph A. Komonchak (Maryknoll, NY: Orbis Books, 1997), 14–19.

the closing of the Second Vatican Ecumenical Council. The Church feels a great need to keep this event alive. With the Council, the Church entered a new phase of her history. The Council Fathers strongly perceived, as a true breath of the Holy Spirit, a need to talk about God to men and women of their time in a more accessible way. The walls which for too long had made the Church a kind of fortress were torn down and the time had come to proclaim the Gospel in a new way. It was a new phase of the same evangelization that had existed from the beginning. It was a fresh undertaking for all Christians to bear witness to their faith with greater enthusiasm and conviction. The Church sensed a responsibility to be a living sign of the Father's love in the world. We recall the poignant words of Saint John XXIII when, opening the Council, he indicated the path to follow: "Now the Bride of Christ wishes to use the medicine of mercy rather than taking up arms of severity. . . . The Catholic Church, as she holds high the torch of Catholic truth at this Ecumenical Council, wants to show herself a loving mother to all; patient, kind, moved by compassion and goodness toward her separated children." (*MV*, no. 4)

And, since *Evangelii Gaudium*, Francis has continued to stress the parallels between John XXIII and himself.[22]

A Reception in Acts and Gestures

The second way that Francis demonstrates his generative reception of Vatican II is his interpretation of the council as an *act* and not simply as a *collection* of final documents—as a reception in acts and gestures. Francis's pontificate is part of the new papacy shaped by Vatican II together with the new global media

---

[22] It is interesting to see that Vatican II is very present in the final document of the Aparecida conference of 2007, but in that document (largely the fruit of Bergoglio's crucial role at that CELAM conference) John XXIII is not mentioned. Bergoglio's closeness to Roncalli seems to have been activated, if not caused, by the conclave of 2013. Francis quotes John XXIII's theological testament and last encyclical, *Pacem in Terris* (April 11, 1963), in the beginning of *Laudato Si'* (no. 3).

culture, globalization of religion, and the comeback of religion in international affairs. In this sense Francis's pontificate is not phenomenically different from the "magisterium of gestures" of his predecessors, at least since John XXIII. But there are gestures that speak specifically to Francis's global reception of the message of Vatican II:

- The washing of the feet of a young Muslim woman prisoner in March 2013. Francis's reception of Vatican II as an act is key to understanding his pontificate as rejection of a neo-exclusivist Catholic ecclesiology.

- His visit to the island of Lampedusa in the Mediterranean Sea on July 8, 2013, to commemorate thousands of migrants who have died crossing the sea, as a sign of a church attentive to the signs of our times;

- The decision to open the Extraordinary Jubilee of Mercy on November 29, 2015, in Bangui, the Central African Republic, as a sign of a church decentralizing from Rome;

- The visit to migrants and refugees detained on the Greek Island of Lesbos on April 16, 2016, as a sign of the ecumenical engagement of the churches on the humanitarian crisis of our time.[23]

Gaudium et Spes plays a special role in the textual as well as the non-textual, performative reception of Vatican II in Francis's pontificate, beginning with the trip to the island of Lampedusa in July 2013. But the textual reception of *Gaudium et Spes* constitutes an important part of his teaching for the effort of *re-contextualization* of the church against the current *de-contextualization* (ideologization and virtualization of the faith experience), and also in terms of re-contextualization of the church's teaching in its own tradition: different moments and different voices. In this respect the use of Vatican II documents in *Amoris Laetitia* cannot be examined without a careful look at the complex relations among different sources: the systematic recourse to Jesus's preaching of the gospel; the tradition of the

---

[23] See Gerard Mannion, *Ecclesiology and Postmodernity: Questions for the Church in Our Time* (Collegeville, MN: Liturgical Press, 2007).

church, especially the papal teaching of the twentieth century; and the post–Vatican II teaching of the bishops' conferences. Francis's non-textual reception of Vatican II is found not only in personal gestures, but also in institutional acts. In Francis's pontificate the most interesting reception of Vatican II as an act has surely been the synodal process of 2014 and 2015 leading to the exhortation *Amoris Laetitia*. It is telling of Francis's reception of Vatican II that *Amoris Laetitia* relies heavily and creatively on the two 2014 and 2015 synodal final reports. Francis chose which texts of the final reports he wanted to quote, and he clearly takes risks with regard to his opposition, making clear his mind and his ecclesiology. Francis quotes from the three paragraphs of the final 2015 report that received the highest number of negative votes.[24] They are significantly used for *Amoris Laetitia*'s section on the pastoral accompaniment of difficult situations. But all this is in the context of a reception of the synodal process that follows the intention of Vatican II for the Synod of Bishops as a body effectively representing the church through the episcopate.

Ecumenism and the New Signs of Our Times

The third demonstration of Francis's generative reception of the council is his understanding of the message of Vatican II *according to the new signs of our times*. This is evident in the example of the "ecumenism of blood," which Francis has talked about from the beginning of his pontificate. There is an ecumenical landscape that has changed tragically as a consequence of the wars that target religious minorities—Christians included—in Africa, the Middle East, and Asia. What Francis calls the ecumenism of blood is certainly part of his ecumenical outlook, as he has said many times, especially in his December 2013 interview with Italian journalist Andrea Tornielli:

> For me, ecumenism is a priority. Today there is an ecumenism of blood. In some countries they kill Christians because they wear a cross or have a Bible, and before killing them

---

[24] No. 84 (72 no votes), no. 85 (80 no votes), and no. 86 (64 no votes).

they don't ask if they're Anglicans, Lutherans, Catholic or Orthodox. Their blood is mixed together. For those who kill, we're Christians. . . . That's the ecumenism of blood. It exists today too, all you have to do is read the papers.[25]

But it is also evident in Francis's reception of the theological message of Vatican II on ecumenism and religious freedom, with the conciliar intuition of the need for a deeper look at the signs of our times, in an intertextual reception of the council.

This has made Francis a global spokesperson for the defense of the religious freedom of persecuted minorities, such as the Rohingya Muslims in Myanmar,[26] and also a general spokesperson for a Catholic Church that is not concerned about its particular position in the world but about being able to advocate for causes that concern the human person today.

Conclusions

Scholars of Vatican II saw in the election of Jorge Mario Bergoglio to the papacy something that eluded those who had dismissed the council as an anomaly in the way Catholicism works. Words, symbols, and acts of the 2013 conclave and of the beginning of Francis's pontificate were clearly an echo of the 1958 conclave and of the beginning of John XXIII's pontificate.[27]

There is something especially relevant in this moment of reception of Vatican II at fifty years, that is, a fundamental shift in the status of the council as a point of reference for Catholic theologians and church leaders. There is no question that all

---

[25] See Andrea Tornielli, interviewer, "'Never Be Afraid of Tenderness'—Pope Francis Interview with *La Stampa*," December 16, 2013.

[26] "Sad news has reached us of the persecution of the religious minority, our Rohingya brothers and sisters. . . . Let us all ask the Lord to save them, and to inspire men and women of good will to come to their aid, so that they may be given their full rights" (Pope Francis, "Angelus" prayer of Sunday, August 27, 2017).

[27] See Massimo Faggioli, *A Council for the Global Church: Receiving Vatican II in History* (Minneapolis: Fortress Press, 2015), esp. 329–35.

the successors of John XXIII were "Vatican II popes" (Paul VI brought the council to a conclusion; John Paul I and John Paul II were council fathers; and Benedict XVI was one of the most important theological *periti* at the council).

But the election of Francis on March 13, 2013, has indubitably changed the landscape of the church and especially of the debate on Vatican II. The fact that Francis is a Vatican II Catholic—and, in a sense, the first post–Vatican II pope—has changed the nature of the debate on the council.

This means also the liberation of papal magisterium from the need to incorporate some of the arguments of the anti-conciliar traditionalist narrative on Vatican II. One can see this from the apostolic letter published motu proprio on January 19, 2019, to decommission the Pontifical Commission *Ecclesia Dei* created by John Paul II in 1988 and to assign its role to a section within the Congregation for the Doctrine of the Faith. This is one of the most important changes Francis has made to the structure of the Roman Curia, and it is particularly interesting because it is a change from the decision made by John Paul II for the discussions with the Society of St. Pius X (SSPX), and from Benedict XVI, who gave the commission a role that it did not have previously under John Paul II. This decision by Francis is important because it reframes the relationship with the SSPX but also with the fragmented world of Catholic post– and anti–Vatican II traditionalism in general. The apostolic letter constituted an interesting disclosure by Francis about how he saw the traditionalist issue in the church and how he interpreted the changes between Benedict XVI's *Summorum Pontificum*, the motu proprio on the liturgy of July 2007, and today. On the one hand, Francis decided that Rome has given the anti-conciliar group SSPX what could possibly be given in terms of normalization of relations; what cannot be given away is the doctrine, that is, Vatican II, which has always been rejected by the SSPX as a legitimate council of the Catholic Church. This is where Francis's decision makes an impact beyond the SSPX and on those Catholics who hoped that the Pontifical Commission *Ecclesia Dei* could bring a traditionalist shift into Rome. The concessions that Francis cannot make to the SSPX about reversing Vatican II are also concessions that he cannot make to traditionalists in communion with Rome. Francis's decision means that the traditionalists can have the preconciliar liturgy, but cannot have an anti-conciliar doctrine sustaining the preconciliar liturgy. This is true for both the SSPX and the traditionalists in communion with Rome. The motu proprio that decommissioned the Pontifical Commission *Ecclesia Dei* is one of the clearest statements of this pontificate on the doctrinal trajectory that the pope has in mind for the Catholic Church. Francis knows that theological and liturgical traditionalism is not going away from Catholicism any time soon. But what is also typical of Francis is the idea that the interpretation of Vatican II as an exercise of textual exegesis made in a historical vacuum is not only a reduction of its meaning, but it is also the subtlest form of rejection of the council. The same form of rejection can be seen in those attempts to interpret Francis's papacy outside of the history of the hermeneutics of Vatican II as an act and not just as a series of documents.

3

Catholicism from the Peripheries

The Pope and the City:
Spiritual Geography of Francis

Popes have a spiritual and intellectual biography that is relevant for understanding their personality and their pontificate. But they also have a spiritual and intellectual *geography*. As the papacy develops in time as an institution, as a position of power that need not be European by default and held by a European clergy, the geography of Catholicism changes as well.

Changes in the geography of the church have an impact on the personality of the popes as well, because the papacy reflects the massive changes in the church but at the same time also interprets these changes. Despite the vast amount of information available on the pope thanks to the mass media, understanding this interpretive aspect of the pontificate has become paradoxically more difficult. Understanding Francis's pontificate requires a sense of time and space and place in a church that is more and more invaded by virtuality. This is even truer when we talk about that particular parallel church of today, that is, the cyberspace of religion, especially the Catholic cyberspace.[1] But there is a new spatiality that is typical of Francis's global pontificate. One of the

---

[1] See Antonio Spadaro, *Cybertheology: Thinking Christianity in the Era of the Internet,* trans. Maria Way (New York: Fordham University Press, 2014); and Massimo Faggioli, "Catholic Cyber-militias and the New Censorship," *La Croix International,* September 18, 2017.

many ways that Francis has re-signified the papacy and Roman Catholicism has been through a profound sense of space—in the *urbs*, the city of Rome, and in the *orbis*, the global world. Geography was important also for the other Francis, Saint Francis of Assisi, whose popularity is linked in a unique way to a series of physical spaces and places: from Assisi and La Verna in central Italy, to the Holy Land and the Middle East for his encounter with Malek al-Kamil, the sultan of Egypt in 1219, during the fifth crusade. The *Italianità* (Italianness) of Francis of Assisi played a particular and controversial role when in 1939, during the Fascist regime, he was proclaimed by Pius XII patron saint of Italy along with Saint Catherine of Siena.

Today the biographical dimension of Jorge Mario Bergoglio translates into a particular sense of space that is new for a pope in the history of modern Catholicism. A son of Italian emigrants, Francis not only has a more direct grasp of the experience of the trauma of displacement, but also of the complexification of the link between place and identity, and of the meaning of this complexification for religious, Christian, and Catholic identity.

He is a pope from Argentina, and the spiritual geography of the new pope became an integral part of the pontificate from the first few moments—a pope from "the end of the world," as he said in his first address to the people in Saint Peter's Square immediately after his election the evening of March 13, 2013. Francis's background from Argentina is peripheral in the historical geography of Catholicism compared to his predecessors on the throne of Peter. This has had an impact, from the beginning of the pontificate, on his way of dealing with the transition from archbishop of Buenos Aires to bishop of Rome and pope of the Catholic Church. For instance, the decision not to live in the papal apartment should not be understood only as a sign of humility, but also as a symbolic re-inculturation of the papacy, beginning with the physical and geographical spaces it occupies. This re-inculturation is especially significant and visible in a city like Rome, which has been re-signified many times but in the early modern period especially was built to be a court, a theater, and a stage for the papacy and the church.[2]

---

[2] See, for example, *Rome, l'unique objet de mon ressentiment. Regards critiques sur la papauté*, ed. Philippe Levillain (Rome: École

The bishop of Rome elected in 2013 was never part of that Roman court and stage, a stark departure from his predecessors in the modern history of Catholicism. Indeed, Jorge Mario Bergoglio had even spent some time in a sort of internal exile from his church and his religious order, the Jesuits, in Cordoba, Argentina.[3] Later, as archbishop, a fundamental experience for Bergoglio was to get out and go to the peripheries of his diocese; this enabled him to develop "a theology of the city that is rather rare in contemporary Catholicism."[4] His role as an outsider was part of his Argentinian life, as it is for his Roman life. He is an outsider in Rome; a stranger to its particular ecclesial, clerical, and curial sociability, with no Roman circle or milieu in his pre-papal life because he was never a student or professor in a Roman university and had never worked in Rome as a Curia official.

Francis's favorite places to meet people and spend time are not the same as those of his predecessors, even the immediate predecessors on the throne of Peter. As bishop of Rome he has almost drawn a new map, one that is very different from the traditional map of papal power in the "holy city" created and solidified between the Renaissance and the Baroque period. It was during this period that the image of Rome was rebuilt after the end of the Great Western Schism, and the papal court was reconstituted during the first half of the fifteenth century, a crucial transitional period for the city's rebirth.[5]

Française de Rome, 2011); and Maria Antonietta Visceglia, *La città rituale. Roma e le sue cerimonie in età moderna* (Rome: Viella, 2002).

[3] See Paul Vallely, *Pope Francis: The Struggle for the Soul of Catholicism* (New York: Bloomsbury, 2015), 111–25.

[4] Andrea Riccardi, *To the Margins: Pope Francis and the Mission of the Church*, trans. Dinah Livingstone (Maryknoll, NY: Orbis Books, 2018), 2, original in Italian, *Periferie. Crisi e novità per la Chiesa* (Milan: Jaca Book, 2016), 8.

[5] See, for example, Gianvittorio Signorotto and Maria Antonietta Visceglia, eds., *Court and Papal Politics in Papal Rome, 1492–1700* (Cambridge, UK: Cambridge University Press, 2002); Günther Wassilowsky and Hubert Wolf, eds., *Werte und Symbole im frühneuzeitlichen Rom* (Darmstadt: Rhema, 2005); and Elizabeth McCahill, *Reviving the Eternal City: Rome and the Papal Court, 1420–1447* (Cambridge, MA: Harvard University Press, 2013).

In the recent history of Rome the label *holy city* had often been used for political-ecclesiastical operations that were very far from Francis's view of politics—from the "conciliation" between the Holy See and the Fascist regime in 1929 to the maneuvering to elect a far-right mayor for Rome in 1952. Francis has discarded the vestiges of the imperial and political papacy (such as the red shoes and the summer residence in Castel Gandolfo) and is bringing Rome much closer to becoming a truly holy city, one that gets the bishop of Rome closer to the immigrants and refugees, to the prison inmates, and to the marginalized.[6] The geography of Francis's action is much more focused on prisons, hospitals, slums, and refugee camps than it is on pontifical universities and academies and the halls of ecclesiastical and political power of the city capital of Italy and the central government of Roman Catholicism. Unlike his predecessors (until Benedict XVI), Francis has never used the papal palace of Castel Gandolfo (sixteen miles from Rome), acquired by the papacy in 1596. In fact, in 2016 Francis decided to turn that summer residence into a museum.

The decentralization of the church with the election of the pope from Argentina coincided with the de-centralization of Italy from the international scene in a geopolitical shift of power toward other European countries (especially Germany) and other areas of the world (especially Asia). Francis came to Rome when it was very evident that the city was transitioning from one of the capitals of the world to one of the many peripheries of the world of politics and of religion. At the same time Francis is being faithful to the special genius of Rome related to the geography of the Italian peninsula and the contradictory identities of the capital city: sacred and profane, religious and anticlerical, glamorous and surrounded by poverty, admired and reviled. It is not only the city of Rome—whose relationship with the papacy has historically fluctuated significantly from a warm embrace to threats against the physical safety of the pope[7]—but it is also the Italian

---

[6] See Andrea Riccardi, *Roma città sacra? Dalla Conciliazione all'operazione Sturzo* (Milan: Vita e pensiero, 1979).

[7] See, for example, David I. Kertzer, *The Pope Who Would Be King: The Exile of Pius IX and the Emergence of Modern Europe* (New York: Random House, 2018).

peninsula. Francis is a pope whose map of Italy is significantly different from that of his predecessors. From his first trip outside Rome in July 2013 to the island of Lampedusa, Francis prefers to visit peripheral but symbolically important places rather than big cities. For example, he traveled to the small cemeteries of Bozzolo and Barbiana in Northern and Central Italy on June 20, 2017, where two important Italian priests for twentieth-century Italian Catholicism, Fr. Primo Mazzolari and Fr. Lorenzo Milani, were buried. Francis was not only the first pope but also the first prelate to acknowledge publicly the contribution of these two priests, whose relations with the institutional church were marked by tensions and marginalization despite their obedience to authorities. The new spiritual geography of the papacy could also be seen in the town of Nomadelfia in Tuscany, where, on May 10, 2018, Francis visited the community of families started there in 1947 by Fr. Zeno Saltini, one of the many priests inspired by the "holy madness" of priests ministering in the peripheries of twentieth-century Italian Catholicism.[8]

Francis wants to be physically close to the forgotten stages of the human drama in the geography of the world of today, and the peripheries of Italy offered opportunities to convey his message early in his pontificate. As he said in his homily in Lampedusa on July 8, 2013, as the first bishop in Italy to visit that tragic landing point between the South and the North of the world, between Europe, Africa, and the Middle East: "So I felt that I had to come here today, to pray and to offer a sign of my closeness, but also to challenge our consciences lest this tragedy be repeated."

Francis has not only redesigned the boundaries of the papal map but also his maps of Europe and of the world. The countries and cities he chooses to visit speak volumes about his priorities. The new map of Pope Francis comes from "Magellan's gaze," which forces us to look at the center from the periphery.[9] His pontificate has intentionally made it impossible to reduce or

---

[8] See Enrico Galavotti and Federico Ruozzi, eds., *"In santità ostinata e incontraria". Don Zeno e i "matti di Dio"* (Bologna: Il Mulino, 2018).

[9] See Antonio Spadaro, "Lo sguardo di Magellano. L'Europa, Papa Francesco, e il Premio Carlo Magno," *Civiltà Cattolica*, 3983 (June 11, 2016): 469–79.

identify its agenda as this or that part of the North American, Latin American, or European Catholic Church. Francis's pontificate also represents a new trajectory for the development of global Catholicism, which spread between the nineteenth and twentieth centuries from the north toward the southern hemisphere, thanks to the missionaries (often supported by colonialism) and the Vatican Sacred Congregation for the Propagation of the Faith.[10] Francis's attention to the peripheries puts into question a Rome-centered view of the church, a view that had already begun to dissolve.

Liminality and Globalization: Francis's Turn to the Peripheries and the Marginalized

Francis's liminality, his being on the border (Latin *limes*) between the old and the new, is determined by his Latin American background, his coming from a family of Italian immigrants to South America, and the particular moment that his pontificate represents in the history of the papacy. Francis did not distance himself from this particular aspect of his biography for fear of destabilizing the papal office. On the contrary, Francis has turned this into a particular attention to the peripheries and the marginalized in a complex articulation of an "explicit and implicit topology," a particular mapping and naming of the sources of his way of doing theology: it is explicit in his drawing from the popular piety of Catholics on the margins, and it is implicit in his drawing from forms of believing and thinking of the people of God.[11]

Francis has used the concept of peripheries from the beginning of his pontificate as a metaphor for social marginality related to the political and economic system rather than the ecclesial.[12]

---

[10] See Riccardi, *To the Margins*, 12–13.

[11] See Michael Quisinsky, "Prolegomena einer Theologie als Lebenswissenschaft 'auf der Grenze.' Papst Franziskus und die theologische Erkenntnislehre," *Theologie und Glaube* 107 (2017): 137–56, esp. 139–44.

[12] See Pasquale Ferrara, "The Concept of Periphery in Pope Francis' Discourse: A Religious Alternative to Globalization?" in *Religions* 6, no. 1 (March 2015): 42–57.

The encounter with the marginalized calls for more responsibility on the part of the Christian community. Francis encourages Christians not to marginalize the sick, the poor, the outcast social sinners. A major moment in the making of Francis's opposition was when, during the in-flight press conference back from the trip to Brazil on July 28, 2013, the pope talked about gays as marginalized. For Francis, marginalization is a spiritual and ecclesial temptation and therefore also a theological issue. He talked about this in his homily during the mass with new cardinals created at consistory, on February 15, 2015, when he spoke about Jesus's gospel as a "reinstatement" of the marginalized: "*Compassion* leads Jesus to concrete action: *he reinstates the marginalized!* These are the three key concepts that the church proposes in today's liturgy of the word: the *compassion* of Jesus in the face of *marginalization* and his desire to *reinstate*."

Francis's turn to the peripheries and the marginalized in Catholicism therefore started early in his pontificate. His three major documents can and must be read through this lens of a de-centering of the pope and of the magisterium toward new outposts of the church, which he describes as a "field hospital."[13]

Evangelii Gaudium from its very title echoes the two most important documents issued between Vatican II and the first post–Vatican II period about the church in the modern world: the constitution *Gaudium et Spes* (1965) and Paul VI's post-synodal exhortation *Evangelii Nuntiandi* (1975). Chapter 1 of *Evangelii Gaudium* is titled "The Church's Missionary Transformation." As never before, Francis's missionary ecclesiology implies a repositioning on the global map and in the local communities—not only a geographical repositioning but also a new posture:

> Let us go forth, then, let us go forth to offer everyone the life of Jesus Christ. Here I repeat for the entire Church what I have often said to the priests and laity of Buenos Aires: I prefer a Church which is bruised, hurting and dirty because it has been out on the streets, rather than a Church which is unhealthy from being confined and from clinging to its own security. I do not want a Church concerned with

---

[13] See Antonio Spadaro, "A Big Heart Open to God," *America* (September 19, 2013).

being at the centre and which then ends by being caught up in a web of obsessions and procedures. (*EG*, no. 49)

Francis analyzes the concrete web of existence and its meaning for the activity of the church, and in a section of his first exhortation outlines a theology for the city in a section titled "Challenges from urban cultures" (*EG*, nos. 71–75). The church has a place and a space in the multicultural city: "Various subcultures exist side by side, and often practise segregation and violence. The church is called to be at the service of a difficult dialogue" (*EG*, no. 74). There is a stark assessment of the human landscape of the cities, but at the same time a sense of how difficult it is to make the post-urban and suburban lifestyle compatible with a life in a Christian community:

We cannot ignore the fact that in cities human trafficking, the narcotics trade, the abuse and exploitation of minors, the abandonment of the elderly and infirm, and various forms of corruption and criminal activity take place. At the same time, what could be significant places of encounter and solidarity often become places of isolation and mutual distrust. Houses and neighborhoods are more often built to isolate and protect than to connect and integrate. (*EG*, no. 75)

Francis's look at the interconnected world of today is not nostalgic for a communitarian, pre-modern Christendom but aware of the challenges and opportunities for fraternity and solidarity:

Today, when the networks and means of human communication have made unprecedented advances, we sense the challenge of finding and sharing a "mystique" of living together, of mingling and encounter, of embracing and supporting one another, of stepping into this flood tide which, while chaotic, can become a genuine experience of fraternity, a caravan of solidarity, a sacred pilgrimage. Greater possibilities for communication thus turn into greater possibilities for encounter and solidarity for everyone. (*EG*, no. 87)

His emphasis on the peripheries means also a redefinition of boundaries and borders. The boundary is the line along which two borders touch each other. In Latin *cum-finis*, "encompassing the end," the border distinguishes by uniting, and thus establishes a connection. Once the boundary is determined, a contact is established. The border is never just a *limes* (in Latin, rigid frontier) but always also *limen* (in Latin, threshold). The liminality of Francis's pontificate lies in his reinterpretation of the borders in this age of new walls. No boundary can therefore claim to exclude "the other," since the boundary by definition implies the "other." The border, by limiting, also relates. Here we find the criterion for escaping the Manichaean confrontation in which we are enmeshed today. Openness and rejection of openness define a relationship that must be painstakingly renegotiated and regained over and over again.

Francis's pastoral and ecclesiological imaginary is both rooted in the native place of and open to the mobility typical of a Jesuit:

> We need to sink our roots deeper into the fertile soil and history of our native place, which is a gift of God. We can work on a small scale, in our own neighborhood, but with a larger perspective. Nor do people who wholeheartedly enter into the life of a community need to lose their individualism or hide their identity; instead, they receive new impulses to personal growth. The global need not stifle, nor the particular prove barren. (*EG*, no. 235)

The social-theological repositioning of the church by Francis is visible in *Laudato Si'*, which, from its very title, *On Care for Our Common Home*, implies a reciprocal interdependence where relations are assumed as an integral part of reality and in which fraternity is made into a priority. The encyclical is addressed to "every person living on this planet" (no. 3). The repositioning is represented in this document by numerous quotations of documents of national and continental bishops' conferences. The papal teaching is repositioned to look at the peripheries as it proposes "paths of liberation":

Furthermore, although this Encyclical welcomes dialogue with everyone so that together we can seek paths of liberation, I would like from the outset to show how faith convictions can offer Christians, and some other believers as well, ample motivation to care for nature and for the most vulnerable of their brothers and sisters. (*LS*, no. 64)

Francis's new choice of the periphery as the place for the voice of the church has precise consequences on the language of the message and also for the recipients of the message. The preferential option for the poor receives a new impulse that is non-ideological but rooted in the departure of Catholicism from a social-political identity that for a long time was assumed to be Western, upper class, middle class, and the poor working class.

At times we see an obsession with denying any pre-eminence to the human person; more zeal is shown in protecting other species than in defending the dignity which all human beings share in equal measure. Certainly, we should be concerned lest other living beings be treated irresponsibly. But we should be particularly indignant at the enormous inequalities in our midst, whereby we continue to tolerate some considering themselves more worthy than others. We fail to see that some are mired in desperate and degrading poverty, with no way out, while others have not the faintest idea of what to do with their possessions, vainly showing off their supposed superiority and leaving behind them so much waste which, if it were the case everywhere, would destroy the planet. In practice, we continue to tolerate that some consider themselves more human than others, as if they had been born with greater rights. (*LS*, no. 90)

This repositioning of the church also entails a non-ideological assessment of the common good in terms of the keepers of the common good. Francis is not afraid of identifying in the secular state a key actor among those who are in charge of promoting and defending the common good, in a clear dissonance from the retreatist and communitarian (if not sectarian) instincts of neo-orthodox or radical orthodox Catholic political theology.[14]

> Underlying the principle of the common good is respect for the human person as such, endowed with basic and inalienable rights ordered to his or her integral development. It has also to do with the overall welfare of society and the development of a variety of intermediate groups, applying the principle of subsidiarity. Outstanding among those groups is the family, as the basic cell of society. Finally, the common good calls for social peace, the stability and security provided by a certain order which cannot be achieved without particular concern for distributive justice; whenever this is violated, violence always ensues. Society as a whole, and the state in particular, are obliged to defend and promote the common good. (LS, no. 157)[15]

This liminal and peripheral turn of the church means also a repositioning in Francis's imaginary of other actors in the world of this time: church, state, and society are not seen in a Christendom-like scenario of subjection of state and society to the church, but squarely in a Vatican II and post–Vatican II worldview where the "marginal Jew"[16] Jesus Christ and his relationship with the social and geographical peripheries of his time have become more paradigmatic than before for the Roman papacy.

The opening of Pope Francis to liminal and peripheral members of the church and of our society did not end at the apparently impassable divide of bio-political issues. From the very beginning of the pontificate the boundaries of the Catholic communion have expanded toward a redefinition of the inclusiveness and exclusiveness of the church. Embracing the liminal

---

[14] See Massimo Faggioli, *Catholicism and Citizenship: Political Cultures of Catholicism in the Twenty-First Century* (Collegeville, MN: Liturgical Press, 2017), 46–66.

[15] See also the section "Dialogue for New National and Local Policies" in *Laudato Si'*, nos. 176–81.

[16] See John P. Meier, *A Marginal Jew: Rethinking the Historical Jesus*, 5 vols. (New Haven, CT: Yale University Press, 1991–2015).

and peripheral condition of many Catholics in "irregular situations" became a focus of Francis before the calling of the bishops' synods of 2014 and 2015, and before the publication of the exhortation *Amoris Laetitia*. For example, in *Evangelii Gaudium*, he writes: "I prefer a Church which is bruised, hurting and dirty because it has been out on the streets, rather than a Church which is unhealthy from being confined and from clinging to its own security" (*EG*, no. 49). But with the publication of *Amoris Laetitia* in April 2016 Francis showed even more clearly his intention to open a new way for the church into this liminality.[17]

Francis's decision about the bishops' synods of 2014 and 2015—from the decision to call them to the post-synodal exhortation *Amoris Laetitia*—has been one of the most consequential of his pontificate thus far, because it has positioned the papacy itself away from the perceived political-moral "center" identified with the magisterium of his two predecessors. The course correction from Benedict's ecclesiology of "creative minorities"[18] entails for Francis also a reconsideration of the criteria for the informal excommunications declared for less-than-ideal Catholics during these last few decades. Francis's exhortation calls for a new approach, especially toward the divorced and remarried (*AL*, nos. 241–46) and, with much less success, toward LGBT Catholics (*AL*, nos. 250–51). It talks about a "logic of integration" (*AL*, no. 299) and of a "discernment [that] is dynamic" (*AL*, no. 303) that are part of the risks of getting the church "bruised, hurting and dirty because it has been out on the streets." But this reach of Francis to liminal and peripheral Catholics begins from the self-understanding of the new place of the papal magisterium in the global church:

> I would make it clear that not all discussions of doctrinal, moral or pastoral issues need to be settled by interventions

---

[17] About this, see Antonio Spadaro, "'Amoris Laetitia'. Struttura e significato dell'Esortazione Apostolica post-sinodale di papa Francesco," *Civiltà Cattolica*, 3980 (April 2, 2016): 105–28.

[18] For Benedict XVI's ecclesiology of the "creative minorities" in the context of secularization, see Massimo Faggioli, *Sorting Out Catholicism: Brief History of the New Ecclesial Movements* (Collegeville, MN: Liturgical Press, 2014), 127–44.

of the magisterium. Unity of teaching and practice is certainly necessary in the Church, but this does not preclude various ways of interpreting some aspects of that teaching or drawing certain consequences from it. This will always be the case as the Spirit guides us towards the entire truth (cf. *Jn* 16:13), until he leads us fully into the mystery of Christ and enables us to see all things as he does. Each country or region, moreover, can seek solutions better suited to its culture and sensitive to its traditions and local needs. For "cultures are in fact quite diverse and every general principle . . . needs to be inculturated, if it is to be respected and applied." (*AL,* no. 3)

The pastoral care of liminal Catholics requires a new liminality of the papal ministry, not only symbolically, but also magisterially, in terms of the position of the papal magisterium in the process of receiving and contributing to the tradition. The function of the bishop of Rome has become one of representation, synthesis, and exegesis of the deep spiritual movements within the global church, and not one of institutional leadership of a propositional Catholicism.

The way Francis understood and celebrated the Extraordinary Jubilee of Mercy of 2015–16 was indicative of this new idea of the relationship between the papal office and the new spiritual and physical geography of the global church. The apparent and deceptive surrender of the Argentinian pope to one of the most controversial institutions of the Roman Catholic Church, a totally medieval invention like the Jubilee, served a key function for Francis's pontificate: establishing a new emphasis on mercy and a new definition of what counts as center and as periphery in the global Catholic Church.[19] This was accomplished, perhaps most visibly, by Francis's geographical choices: he opened the Jubilee in Bangui, in the Central African Republic; the places of the most important celebrations of the Jubilee in Rome were not in Saint Peter's Basilica or in other classic places of papal Rome but were instead part of

---

[19] About Francis's interpretation and intention for the Extraordinary Jubilee of Mercy, see Alberto Melloni, *Il giubileo. Una storia* (Rome-Bari: Laterza, 2015), 109–28.

the "Fridays of Mercy" (which continued after the end of the
Jubilee), when Francis visited hospitals, elder care facilities,
prisons, detention camps for refugees, and the families, wives,
and children of priests who had left the ordained ministry.

Francis's World and North America

This new spiritual and physical geography of the global church
as interpreted by Francis constitutes a challenge for the geopolitical atlas of all Catholics, and in particular for Catholicism
in North America. It is not just a political tension between the
message of Francis and the majority of white Catholics in the
United States who helped elect Donald Trump to the presidency
in November 2016. There is a more profound contradiction
and a tension between the pontificate of Francis and recent tendencies of ecclesiology in North America—including Catholic
ecclesiology—tempted by the option of radical withdrawal from
the public scene in order to found Christian communities of
the neo-monastic or otherwise sectarian type. These tendencies
signal the attempt to rebuild a majority-complex Christianity in
small communities. This attempt to seclude Christianity aims at
separating Christian life from contemporary cultural and religious moral pluralism as a reaction against the epochal defeat
suffered by conservative Christianity in "culture wars" from
the 1970s to today. On the one hand, Francis has proposed,
from the beginning of his pontificate, a much wider agenda
than that of cultural wars on sexual norms. On the other hand,
Francis's ecclesiology rejects any form of neo-Constantinianism
and pre–Vatican II political Augustinianism, which presupposes
a superior legitimacy for the role of the church in relation to
politics. All this implies a gap between Francis's and the neoconservative and neo-integralist conceptions of the space of the
church in our world and society: the church not in terms of
"who," of its identity, but in terms of "where."[20] The Catholic

---

[20] For the relationship between the ecclesiology of Vatican II and
the "where" of the Catholic Church, see the commentary to *Gaudium
et Spes*: Hans-Joachim Sander, "Theologischer Kommentar zur Pas-
toralkonstitution über die Kirche in der Welt von heute," in *Herders*

Church of the culture wars relies on a spiritual geography, on a sense of space and place, that is not the same as that lifted up by Francis.

The most visible element of tension between the atlas of Francis and that of North America and of the Western world in our time is the role of the human in a world caught up in the epochal crisis of migrants and refugees—again, a tension connected to spatial imagination. Francis—as a citizen, a priest, a Jesuit, and a bishop close to migrants and refugees—sees the church and the world in a process of global resettlement. Here Francis's pontificate must be seen in the long history of the Catholic Church dealing with migrations. Between the late nineteenth and early twentieth centuries the phenomenon of mass migration was more a problem than a resource from the point of view of the Holy See, which had to intervene to settle jurisdictional, liturgical, and international disputes caused by the mass movements of Catholics. "But gradually—and overtly since Vatican II—the hierarchy, itself increasingly composed of non-European bishops, has intervened to set out guidelines for Catholic engagement in matter of mobility. . . . Theology, ecclesiology, and institutional structures have thus coevolved towards a project of universality divulgated in moral, spiritual, diplomatic, or educational terms."[21]

The globalization of Catholicism means the development and more urgent relevance of the papal narrative on migration and mobility, which means a renaissance of the political relevance of the papacy in the world of fractured globalization. But it is also a papacy with fewer means of controlling and imposing the papal narrative on the global church and with more opposition coming from those Catholic churches that find themselves in a new situation of being on the peripheries like all the other Catholic churches, for example, US Catholicism. This is one of the effects of the end of a Rome-controlled globalization of Catholicism, which is particularly visible in North America because of several

---

Theologischer Kommentar zum Zweiten Vatikanischen Konzil, ed. Bernd Jochen Hilberath and Peter Hünermann, vol. 5 (Freiburg i.Br.: Herder, 2005), 581–886.

[21] Isacco Turina, "Centralized Globalization: The Holy See and Human Mobility since World War II," *Critical Research on Religion* 3, no. 2 (2015): 189–205.

factors: the Catholic Church in the United States plays a unique role in American politics; the United States is a powerful magnet for migrants; and the issue of migration has been one of the defining issues of US domestic politics during the pontificate of Francis.

The Peripheries and the Crisis of Globalization

Francis's pontificate coincides with the increasing visibility of the crisis of economic and political globalization, a crisis that has been called the age of anger, with the resurgence of reactionary, nationalist, isolationist, and chauvinist movements.[22] It is an anger from which global Catholicism cannot claim to be exempt and, on the contrary, is fully part of intra-Catholic tensions today. Catholic anger can be seen in militant members of the church who rail against modernity and the world of today as well as in those self-appointed "orthodox" Catholics who fume at other Catholics. But it is also seen in liberal-progressive Catholics who vent their anger over their unfulfilled hopes for the reform that they expected from the Second Vatican Council, which some saw as their church's equivalent of the Enlightenment.

Francis's papacy has internalized a particular version of this anger; his global view is one of the voices of the Catholic discontent and disillusionment with economic globalization and the inequalities it produces. At the same time, Francis does not reject the cosmopolitan and internationalist worldview of Catholicism articulated during the twentieth century.[23] This is one of the gaps between the rejection of political modernity and of multilateralism by the conservative sectors of American Catholicism (and its political projections) and the view of modernity of Pope Fran-

---

[22] See Pankaj Mishra, *The Age of Anger: A History of the Present* (New York: Farrar, Straus and Giroux, 2017).

[23] See Americo Miranda, *Santa Sede e Società delle Nazioni. Benedetto XV, Pio XI e il nuovo internazionalismo cattolico* (Rome: Studium, 2013); and Jacopo Cellini, *Universalism and Liberation: Italian Catholic Culture and the Idea of International Community 1963–1978* (Leuven: Leuven University Press, 2017).

cis.[24] Francis's criticism of capitalism and economic globalization does not become anti-globalism or anti-internationalism; he has instead articulated a powerful rejection of the ethno-nationalist turn while advocating for just international relations, but without rejecting the international order based on the nation-state and on international organizations founded in the twentieth century.[25]

A new Catholic universalism had already begun to be articulated in a new way in a precise moment in modern Catholicism: in those few weeks between the radio message of John XXIII on September 11, 1962; the opening of the Second Vatican Council on October 11, 1962; and the *Message to Humanity* of October 20, 1962—the first document of the council to the world. In his radio message of September 11, 1962, John XXIII talked about the new way for the church to look at the world: "Looking at the underdeveloped countries, the church introduces itself for what it is, and wants to be: the church of all, and especially the church of the poor." In the opening speech of the council on October 11, 1962, *Gaudet Mater Ecclesia*, John XXIII talked about the unity of the Christian and human family: "The unity of Catholics among themselves, which must always be kept exemplary and most firm; the unity of prayers and ardent desires with which those Christians separated from this Apostolic See aspire to be united with us; and the unity in esteem and respect for the Catholic Church which animates those who follow non-Christian religions."[26] And in the *Message to Humanity* the council fathers started to articulate a theology of the Christian and Catholic engagement in a world no longer perceived as distant or as the enemy:

---

[24] About the accusation that Francis has abandoned early twentieth-century Catholic anti-modernism, see, for example, R. R. Reno, "The Populist Wave Hits the Catholic Church," *Foreign Affairs* (November 13, 2018).

[25] See Francis, *Address to the Diplomatic Corps Accredited to the Holy See*, January 7, 2019.

[26] John XXIII, *Gaudet Mater Ecclesia* (October 11, 1962), in *The Documents of Vatican II*, ed. Walter M. Abbott (London: Chapman, 1966), 717.

Coming together in unity from every nation under the sun, we carry in our hearts the hardships, the bodily and mental distress, the sorrows, longings, and hopes of all the peoples entrusted to us. We urgently turn our thoughts to all the anxieties by which modern man is afflicted. Hence, let our concern swiftly focus first of all on those who are especially lowly, poor, and weak. Like Christ, we would have pity on the multitude weighed down with hunger, misery, and lack of knowledge. We want to fix a steady gaze on those who still lack the opportune help to achieve a way of life worthy of human beings.

As we undertake our work, therefore, we would emphasize whatever concerns the dignity of man, whatever contributes to a genuine community of peoples. "Christ's love impels us," for "he who sees his brother in need and closes his heart against him, how does the love of God abide in him?"[27]

Those words and events of the fall of 1962 play a prominent role in Francis's hermeneutic of Vatican II, especially John XXIII's *Gaudet Mater Ecclesia*. The unfolding of the conciliar experience, especially the experience of the Latin American church at the Second Vatican Council, was marked by the shift to the church of the poor and for the poor: the witness of the bishops and their voice for a church not afraid to embody a radical witness to the gospel not only in a new sense of history, but also in a new ecclesial geography. The signing of the "Catacomb Pact" on November 16, 1965, was the culmination of that conciliar experience, in which the Latin American bishops involved other bishops from other continents (but with little enthusiasm from North American council fathers) in that commitment.[28] Francis's Latin America experience is in itself reshaping the church: "The

---

[27] Vatican II, "Message to Humanity," October 20, 1962, in Abbott, *The Documents of Vatican II*, 5.

[28] For the text of the "Catacomb Pact," the list of signatories, and a historical introduction, see José Oscar Beozzo, *Pacto das catacumbas. Por uma Igreja servidora e pobre* (São Paulo: Paulinas, 2015). The list of signatories comprised nine bishops from Africa, nine from Latin America and Caribe, thirteen from Asia, nine from Europe, one from Israel, and one from North America (the bishop of Saint-Jean-de-Québec, in Canada).

ministry of Francis comes from a periphery that redefines ecclesial relations. . . . This new scenario marks the beginning of the end of ecclesial Eurocentrism, even though some underestimate Latin American Catholicism."[29] Francis's pontificate is preoccupied with the attempt to reverse one of the big shifts that took place in Catholicism between the nineteenth and twentieth centuries: the divorce of clerical culture and of the ecclesiastical institution from the poor, from poverty, in favor of the working class and the working poor. This is a key framework for understanding the attempt as well as the moralistic pushback against the post-bourgeois Christian morality of *Amoris Laetitia* and the attempt to make real space in the church for the complicated social and economic reality of families in the contemporary world.

Francis is not just a Jesuit coming from a vaguely defined global south, but a Jesuit coming from that particular ecclesial experience that made Latin American Catholics look at the world during the post–Vatican II period through the eyes of the poor; the non-institutional Catholicism of Pope Francis is not the same as the anti-institutional sentiment of the late 1960s and 1970s in the northern hemisphere. It is an ecclesiological view of the contradiction not between institutional church and individual freedom, but between institutional church and church of the poor.[30] The canonization of Óscar Romero in 2018 is typical of Francis in the sense that it is an affirming and re-signifying appropriation of the experience of martyrdom by the institutional church, which is often at the heart of the politics of canonizations in the postconciliar church and a matter of debate between those who expect the institutional church to recognize martyrdom with a declaration of sainthood and those who don't want the institution to taint an informally but widely recognized sainthood.[31] Francis makes for the church the connection between the option for the poor and the geography of Catholicism. He does

---

[29] Carlos Maria Galli, "Il forte vento del sud," *Il Regno—attualità* 2 (2014), 60 (English translation mine).

[30] See Andrea Riccardi, *La sorpresa di papa Francesco. Crisi e futuro della Chiesa* (Milan: Mondadori, 2013), 87.

[31] See Kathleen Sprows Cummings, *A Saint of Our Own: How the Quest for a Holy Hero Helped Catholics Become American* (Chapel Hill: University of North Carolina Press, 2019).

so in a situation that is vastly different from the one at the time of the council: a new relationship between the religious and the secular, politics and economy, church and state, and democracy and capitalism.

The Historical and Geographical Shift of Francis's Pontificate

As one of the most original interpreters of twentieth-century Catholicism, the Italian mystic and politician Giorgio La Pira writes, "Christianity is history and geography."[32] Francis's rethinking of Catholicism as from and for the peripheries is part of a more comprehensive historical process going on in the church. This process must be understood as something that Francis embodies objectively as much as he guides and leads it subjectively. Francis's pontificate helps us understand, from the vantage point of the global Catholic Church, the long underestimated role of the Roman papacy to interpret the tectonic shifts in the church and in the world, compared to the post–Vatican I understanding of the papacy as dominated by a charismatic leadership that owes to anti-modern Catholic political culture not less than to the history of the theological tradition on the papacy.[33]

This objective and subjective shift toward a more global understanding of Catholicism can be understood from the vantage point of the gaps between Joseph Ratzinger and Jorge Mario Bergoglio in the context of the periodization of twentieth-century Catholicism. The two popes are separated by less than a decade in their dates of birth (1927 for Ratzinger, 1936 for Bergoglio),

---

[32] See the letters of Giorgio La Pira (1904–77) to the popes, in which he often expressed his historical-geographical vision of the God's plan and a "geography of grace": Giorgio La Pira, *Beatissimo Padre. Lettere a Pio XII*, ed. Andrea Riccardi and Isabella Piersanti (Milan: Mondadori, 2004); *Il sogno di un tempo nuovo. Lettere a Giovanni XXIII*, ed. Andrea Riccardi and Augusto D'Angelo (Cinisello Balsamo: San Paolo, 2009); *Abbattere muri, costruire ponti. Lettere a Paolo VI*, ed. Andrea Riccardi and Augusto D'Angelo (Milan: San Paolo, 2015).

[33] See John W. O'Malley, *Vatican I: The Council and the Making of the Ultramontane Church* (Cambridge, MA: Belknap Press of Harvard University Press, 2018).

but a much longer generation divides them in terms of ecclesial and theological culture. The future Benedict XVI was ordained in 1951, in the early post–*Humani Generis* Catholicism, in Germany, where Catholicism was a pillar of political and cultural stability and one of the most important institutional and symbolical healers of the physical, psychological, cultural, and moral wounds of World War II. The future pope Francis was ordained in 1969, in the early post–Vatican II period, in a Latin American church that was appropriating the council as the birth of a newly global Catholicism at a time of great challenges for the Catholic Church, as it sought to liberate itself from the role of ideological legitimacy of the social and political status quo.

This gap between Benedict and Francis continues if one looks synoptically at their biographies and careers. The year 1969, when Jorge Mario Bergoglio was ordained to the priesthood, was the year that marked the first departure of Joseph Ratzinger from the faculty of theology at the University of Tübingen and, with it, from a certain understanding of progressive Vatican II Catholicism. In Latin America the first effects of the Medellín conference of the CELAM in 1968 began to be felt in the Catholic churches of the continent. In the 1980s and 1990s the marginalization of Jorge Mario Bergoglio from the Jesuits and from his local church familiarized him with the experience of ordinary marginality of Catholics in the peripheries of Argentina. At the same time the Rome of Cardinal Ratzinger, and especially the Congregation for the Doctrine of the Faith, were dealing in unsympathetic terms with the theology of liberation and its Latin American thinkers.

The gap was amplified in the period of the pontificate of Benedict XVI, when Cardinal Archbishop Bergoglio of Buenos Aires, who was the runner-up in the conclave of 2005, observed from "the end of the world" the re-Europeanization of the papacy, of the Roman Curia, and of the doctrinal policy of the Vatican for the global church.[34]

The differences between Benedict XVI and Francis are not limited to the two kinds of Catholicism they represent in their

---

[34] For the sharply different views of the role of Europe for Christianity and the Catholic Church between Francis and Benedict XVI, see Joseph Ratzinger, *Church, Ecumenism, and Politics: New Essays in Ecclesiology* (New York: Crossroad, 1988), esp. 221–36.

unusual cohabitation at the Vatican after the resignation of Benedict XVI. Of course, the effort to understand Francis's pontificate cannot avoid the issue of his relationship with his predecessor. But in order to escape the trap of reducing the shift from Benedict to Francis to some kind of duel between two ideas of church leadership, the effort must be directed at the comprehension of their different historical and geographical worlds; Francis's rethinking of Catholicism as from and for the peripheries entails understanding the tension between the European and Western narrative on the post–Vatican II period, on one hand, and the history of the typical post–Vatican II issues in the global church, on the other.

The gap between Francis and his predecessor has allowed the papacy to become more attentive to massive changes in the church of today. One of the typical post–Vatican II issues that help us understand the shift toward a global Catholicism is the issue of the laity. The Catholic laity today is less European, more global; a laity for which the distinction between laity and clergy no longer subsists in the reception or export of cultural and symbolic aggregates of the European matrix; a laity in which Catholicism is no longer passed down from generation to generation. It is a laity in a church that has become one of the institutions remodeled by the individualization of lifestyles: a swinging door that one can enter and exit several times, remain part of in many different and "liminal" ways, or remain part of Catholic communion at the same time as participation in the life of another church for family reasons (mixed marriages) or for deliberate "contamination" between different confessional identities. It is a church where ideological militancy for a certain kind of Catholicism does not necessarily coincide with a high level of commitment in the church. One of the most visible effects of the globalization of Catholicism is the estrangement of Catholic laity from the original, nineteenth- and twentieth-century mold of the Catholic lay person as a member of the bourgeois middle class. The rise of the laity in ecclesiology and in the Catholic Church between the end of the nineteenth and early twentieth centuries—both theological-systematic as well as sociological and practical—was both cause and effect of the mobilization of the masses and of the democratization in the West, but it was also part of the Catholic response to the mobilization and democratization of the masses in the new nation-states. Now, during Francis's pontificate, the new phase of accelerating de-Europeanization and de-Occidentalization of Catholicism also means a redefinition of relations between the laity as a theological and canonical category, on the one hand, and its identification with the social, economic, and political ideals of European-Western origin, on the other.

Another example of the gap between Francis and the post–Vatican II church is the issue of bio-politics, where we can see the new emphasis of the pontificate on the teachings of the church on marriage, family, and sexuality. The importance of gospel radicalism, of mercy, and of discernment cannot be separated from Francis's radical critique of the contemporary, dominant socioeconomic system in which the moral discourse of both the institution and the individual is framed. On the other hand, the more moderate shift marked by Francis's approach to the issues of gender, homosexual marriage, and women in the church must be viewed in the context of a radical critique of the contemporary, dominant socioeconomic system where equality tends to signify sameness.[35]

The Post–Vatican II Period, Far from Rome

Francis can be seen as the first postconciliar pope, given that he is the first pope who was ordained a priest after the end of Vatican II. But he is also a product of the globalization of Catholicism.[36] His interpretation of Vatican II relies on his global identity as a Latin American Catholic with deep Italian roots;

---

[35] See Giannino Piana, "Il magistero morale di papa Francesco. Tra radicalità e Misericordia," in *Papa Francesco. Quale teologia*, ed. Alberto Cozzi, Roberto Repole, Giannino Piana, afterword Cardinal Gianfranco Ravasi (Assisi: Cittadella, 2016), 127–91.

[36] See Pape François, *Rencontres avec Dominique Wolton. Politique et société. Un dialogue inédit* (Paris: Éditions de l'Observatoire, 2017). In this series of dialogues with the French sociologist Wolton, Francis distinguishes between *globalization* (which destroys the differences, "globalization of indifference") and *mundialization* (a state becoming a "world citizen," that is, a process not seen negatively).

a Jesuit who has consistently absorbed the Society of Jesus's global and pluralistic worldview while developing further intuitions of Vatican II;[37] and a priest who was archbishop of Buenos Aires, the secular and cosmopolitan capital of the massively urbanized global south in the period between the early post–Cold War period and the early post–9/11 and post-American world.

At the same time, from a theological point of view Francis's Catholicism is theologically shaped more by Vatican II Catholicism than by post–Vatican II Catholic theology. In other words, it remains to be seen if and how much the pontificate of Francis will be able to lead the church beyond the magisterial and cultural boundaries of Vatican II on issues that the council did not discuss and did not deal with both in terms of theological-systematic issues and for the institutional reform of the church.

Jesuit historian Stephen Schloesser calls the Vatican II paradigm "dancing on the edge of the volcano":

> The years 1962–1965 stand as a fulcrum. When we look at December 1965 from the political vantage point, the Council appears to have concluded an armistice with modernity. However, looking at the same moment from the biopolitical perspective, the Council seems to have been caught off guard, struggling to keep up with rapid currents outstripping its capacity to make sense. One way of historically interpreting this seeming paradox is that biopolitical issues in 1965 had taken over the recently vacated space once occupied by eighteenth- and nineteenth-century political issues. Even as the Council euphorically celebrated its peace with the past, it unknowingly danced on the edge of a volcano.[38]

---

[37] See Drew Christiansen, "The Global Vision of *Evangelii Gaudium*: Cultural Diversity as a Road to Peace," in *Pope Francis and the Future of Catholicism:* Evangelii Gaudium *and the Papal Agenda*, ed. Gerard Mannion (New York: Cambridge University Press, 2017), 203–20.

[38] Stephen R. Schloesser, "'Dancing on the Edge of the Volcano': Biopolitics and What Happened after Vatican II," in *From Vatican II to Pope Francis: Charting a Catholic Future*, ed. Paul Crowley, SJ, 3–26 (Maryknoll, NY: Orbis Books, 2014), 26.

Francis's caution in dealing with genuinely post–Vatican II theological issues, such as the role of women in the church in terms of women in ministry, is the flip side of his refusal to accept ideological readings of contemporary Catholicism as a tool for a hypocritical "turn to values"—a turn that makes Christianity the chaperone for an ultra-individualized and moralistic political religion. Interpreting Vatican II from the peripheries does not entail necessarily the embrace of a progressive Catholic theology. Globalization is the destiny of Catholicism, but the theological trajectories of globalized Catholicism are difficult to predict.

Francis has proven the point that every counter narrative about Vatican II as the alleged beginning of the decay of Catholicism and of Western civilization because of the embrace of Vatican II for the "western liberal consensus"[39] is a narrative that can proceed only from a Western and North Atlantic political perspective and that makes limited sense historically and theologically for global Catholicism. Francis has shown also a fidelity to the teaching and theology of Vatican II not influenced by the sociopolitical narratives on the post–Vatican II era that dominated the Euro-Western theological debate, especially under Benedict XVI. Francis's pontificate has been marked by a non-ideological and non-nostalgic approach to Vatican II, with a rather cautious use of the council's corpus. Francis's relationship with Vatican II "could be seen as marked by more freedom"[40] in comparison to his predecessors, especially Paul VI and Benedict XVI.

This turn must be seen together with Francis's meta-doctrinal shift—the primacy of the pastoral—that was also the most important theological shift of Vatican II: "The pastorality that marks Vatican II can be defined as the art of giving men and women access to the one source of the Gospel message,"[41] in

---

[39] See the thesis by Richard John Neuhaus, *The Catholic Moment* (San Francisco: Harper and Row, 1987), 37–69.

[40] Christoph Theobald, "L'exhortation apostolique *Evangelii Gaudium*. Esquisse d'une interprétation originale du Concile Vatican II," *Revue Théologique de Louvain* 46 (2015): 326.

[41] Christoph Theobald, *Accéder à la source*, vol. 1 in *La réception du concile Vatican II* (Paris: Cerf, 2009), 697; see also idem, "*Dans les traces . . .*" *de la constitution "Dei Verbum" du Concile Vatican II. Bible, théologie, et pratiques de lecture* (Paris: Cerf, 2009).

our world of postmodernity, where our contemporaries have to face a variety of sources:

> Vatican II was a re-reading of the Gospel in light of contemporary culture. . . . Vatican II produced a renewal movement that simply comes from the same Gospel. Its fruits are enormous. Just recall the liturgy. The work of liturgical reform has been a service to the people as a re-reading of the Gospel from a concrete historical situation. Yes, there are hermeneutics of continuity and discontinuity, but one thing is clear: the dynamic of reading the Gospel, actualizing its message for today—which was typical of Vatican II—is absolutely irreversible.[42]

There is not only a geographical and geopolitical shift in the magisterial reception and interpretation of Vatican II under Francis, but there is also a new relationship between the interpretation of Vatican II and the interpretation of the post–Vatican II period. A different geography of the church implies a different historical interpretation of the recent past, of Vatican II, and especially of the post–Vatican II period, for which there is not yet a universal narrative, much less a universalist interpretation. Under Francis, the whole history of the postconciliar period is interpreted not from the perspective of the myth of medieval Christendom and of the loss of Christendom to secularization,[43] but from the perspective of the emancipation of Catholicism in Latin America precisely from that myth in an appreciation of the secular and of the cosmopolitan that is quite the opposite of the ecclesiastical institutional-hierarchical interpretation of the post–Vatican II period in the United States. If it is true that there is a missiological reframing in Francis from a geographical to a cultural and relational understanding of the missionary activity of the church,[44] there is also a geo-

---

[42] Spadaro, "A Big Heart Open to God."

[43] For the resilience of the myth of medieval Christendom in the twentieth century, see Giovanni Miccoli, *Fra mito della cristianità e secolarizzazione. Studi sul rapporto chiesa-società nell'età contemporanea* (Genoa: Marietti, 1985).

[44] See Theobald, "L'exhortation apostolique *Evangelii Gaudium*," 328.

graphical reframing that is deeply felt and not without angst at the cultural-economic centers of the world, such as those in the United States.

There is not only a vastly different theological appreciation in Francis, compared to Benedict XVI and the generation of bishops appointed by him (as pope and before, thanks to his influence as cardinal prefect of the Congregation for the Doctrine of the Faith between 1982 and 2005), for the fruits of the liturgical reform in relation to the ecclesiology of Vatican II. There is also a different experience of the path of a continental church, the one in Latin America, from the conference of the CELAM in Medellín in 1968 to the conference of Aparecida in 2007.[45] There is a different reception of the pontificate of Paul VI, of the exhortations *Evangelii Nuntiandi* and *Gaudete in Domino* (both 1975), and of the institution of the bishops' synod in general; much of Vatican II and the post–Vatican II era is seen by Francis through a reception of the teachings of Paul VI. *Evangelii Nuntiandi* especially is the mediating source for Francis's *ressourcement* toward Vatican II. As one of the major interpreters of Vatican II, Christoph Theobald, puts it, "Ten years after the end of the council, *Evangelii Nuntiandi* represented the first synthetic re-reading of the corpus of Vatican II."[46] Where there is distance between *Evangelii Nuntiandi* and *Evangelii Gaudium* is in Francis's confidence in a more decentralized Catholic Church (*EG,* no. 32), one of the interrupted trajectories of Vatican II.

Francis comes from an ecclesial and political periphery that redefines intra-ecclesial relations. There is a different evaluation and affirmation of some conciliar and postconciliar theological and ecclesial experiences that until Francis were considered problematic for the institutional church. The overcoming of the postconciliar polarization is not about a new theoretical effort for the interpretation of Vatican II, or about a change in the theological culture of the power holder in the Vatican. It is about opening to the global Catholicity that before

---

[45] See Diego Fares, SJ, "A dieci anni da Aparecida. Alle fonti del pontificato di Francesco," *La Civiltà Cattolica*, 4006 (May 20, 2017): 338–52.

[46] Theobald, "L'exhortation apostolique *Evangelii Gaudium*," 321.

becoming an object of the theological vision of Vatican II was already an active subject of the making of the council. The de-Westernization of the reception of Vatican II is one of the most important things that arrived in Rome with Pope Francis.

4

Ad limina of the Peripheries

Francis's Ecclesiology of Globalization

Pope Francis set out to inaugurate a new ecclesiology of globalization from the beginning of his pontificate, and this theme is a common thread in his message to the church. There are different dimensions in Francis's ecclesiology of globalization. This pontificate represents: (1) a particular, new phase in the long history of the inculturation of the Roman papacy; (2) the attempt to articulate the growing tension between institutional and missionary Catholicism in the global world; (3) a new embodiment of the sociopolitical message of the Catholic Church in its ecclesiology of globalization; and (4) a new elaboration of an ecclesiology of the laity in the new spatiality of the church in globalization.

Catholic Globalization, Ecumenism, and New Inculturation of the Papacy

For Pope Francis, the approach of Catholicism to the issue of globalization and its consequences for the church does not start with a process of bureaucratic reform of the institution, which can be seen as one of the areas in which the pontificate has not invested to the extent many expected and hoped—and others clearly feared. The approach is typically theological and spiritual, but not without institutional consequences. The first visible step of Francis's ecclesiology of globalization was a new inculturation of the papacy, marked by a complex mix of tradition-minded *ressourcement* and of progressive *aggiornamento*. Francis's inculturation of the papacy must be understood in the context of the ecclesiological debate on the future of the papacy in these last few decades as well as in the context of the significant changes in the perception of the Petrine ministry by Catholics and non-Catholics.

Francis's interpretation of the papal ministry follows in the footsteps of John XXIII and Vatican II and echoes the consensus within Catholic ecclesiology of the need for a rediscovery for the third millennium of the role of the papacy established in the first millennium.[1] There are many differences between the papacies of the period between Vatican II and today, on one side, and the papacy of confessionalization in the second millennium, especially after Trent and after Vatican I, on the other side.[2] With the shifts in the Catholic understanding and imagination of the papacy around and after Vatican I, the papacy took on a more ecumenical role and was less defined by the growth of the papal primacy in the Catholic Church between the early second millennium and the nineteenth century. But it is a complex mix. In the nineteenth century the transnational phenomenon of Ultramontanism—a theological-political movement in reaction to Enlightenment rationalism, political liberalism, and the forces of change in the nineteenth century—was a key contribution to the creation of a new global Catholic imagination. After Vatican II it has become clear that the legacy of Ultramontanism for the modern papacy is a genie that is hard to put back in the bottle.[3]

Francis deals with the need to complete the Vatican II task of rebalancing Vatican I and at the same time continues the promise

---

[1] See Joseph Ratzinger, "Prognosen für die Zukunft des Ökumenismus" (1976), in Joseph Ratzinger, *Theologische Prinzipienlehre* (Munich: Wiewel, 1982), 203–14.

[2] For the concept of confessionalization, see Wolfgang Reinhard, "Zwang zur Konfessionalisierung? Prolegomena zu einer Theorie des konfessionellen Zeitalters," *Zeitschrift für historische Forschung* 10 (1983): 257–77.

[3] For the factors leading to Ultramontanism, see John W. O'Malley, *Vatican I: The Council and the Making of the Ultramontane Church* (Cambridge, MA: Harvard University Press, 2018), esp. 55–95.

of Vatican II and of the postconciliar papacies to redefine the Petrine ministry.[4] This is the meaning of the redefinition of the role of the papacy in some of the most important teachings of Francis, who in *Evangelii Gaudium* writes: "It is not advisable for the Pope to take the place of local Bishops in the discernment of every issue which arises in their territory. In this sense, I am conscious of the need to promote a sound 'decentralization'" (*EG*, no. 16). In the opening of *Amoris Laetitia* Francis goes further: "I would make it clear that not all discussions of doctrinal, moral or pastoral issues need to be settled by interventions of the magisterium" (*AL*, no. 3). These are expressions of this ecclesiological *ressourcement*, for which the ecclesiology of Vatican II opened the way not only with the ecclesiological constitution *Lumen Gentium*, but also with the documents on the liturgy, on divine revelation, on ecumenism, and on religious liberty.

But Francis's reform of the papacy is neither an attempt to return to the papacy of the first millennium, nor a return to the ecclesiology of the papacy and episcopacy of the documents of Vatican II. Also on this issue, Francis is more a postconciliar pope than a Vatican II pope as his predecessors were. Francis's approach to the ecclesiology of the papacy in relationship to the globalization of Catholicism owes more to the postconciliar debates on the ecclesiology of the local and universal church than to the letter of the documents of Vatican II or the hermeneutical issues related to Vatican II.[5]

Francis's re-inculturation of the papacy follows the Roman Catholic genius of building on a complex theological and institutional series of layers:

---

[4] See John R. Quinn, *The Reform of the Papacy: The Costly Call to Christian Unity* (New York: Crossroad, 2000); *Changer la papauté?*, ed. Paul Tihon (Paris: Cerf, 2000); *Papstamt und Ökumene. Zum Petrusdienst und der Einheit aller Getauften*, ed. Peter Hünermann (Regensburg: Pustet, 1997); and Hermann J. Pottmeyer, *Die Rolle des Papsttums im Dritten Jahrtausend* (Freiburg i.B.: Herder, 1999).

[5] For the ecclesiological debate between Joseph Ratzinger and Walter Kasper of 1999 and the early 2000s, see Kilian McDonnell, "The Ratzinger/Kasper Debate: The Universal Church and Local Churches," *Theological Studies* (2002): 222–50.

- the Gregorian Reform of the eleventh century, that is, the beginning of a new phase in the relationship between Roman Catholicism and the papacy in the sense of a centralization of the ecclesial and ecclesiastical dynamics of Rome, also in order to implement church reform: in the words of Yves Congar, "Historically, centralization has been a necessity and a good thing."[6]
- Trent, with the growing confessional identification of the papacy and the person of the pope with the effort of church reform in terms of personal purification.[7]
- Vatican I, whose impact on the Catholic Church regarding the papacy was much more about papal primacy than infallibility.[8]
- Vatican II, in the history of the efforts of interpreting and implementing the new "quasi-constitutional" relationship among the papacy, the church, and the world: collegiality (with the bishops), synodality (with the whole church), ecumenism (with the rest of Christianity), interreligious dialogue, and service to humankind.

In different ways all the popes of the last century have contributed to this new formulation of the papal role.[9] Francis's contribution is at the same time a continuation of this development of the tradition on the papacy and a specific contribution to it marked by a particular ecclesiological consciousness of the papacy in this particular moment of globalization of the world, of religion, and of Catholicism. There is not just the clear symbolism of renouncing the Renaissance papacy by renouncing the papal apartment in the Vatican. There is also

---

[6] Yves Congar, *True and False Reform in the Church*, trans. Paul Philibert (Collegeville, MN: Liturgical Press, 2010), original in French (Paris: Cerf, 1950, 1968), 262.

[7] See the shift from the munificence of the popes between the Renaissance and the mid-seventeenth century to the austere papacies of Innocent XI (1676–89) and Innocent XII (1691–1700).

[8] See Klaus Schatz, *Papal Primacy: From Its Origins to the Present* (Collegeville, MN: Liturgical Press, 1996), original in German (Würzburg: Echter, 1990), 155–71.

[9] See Daniele Menozzi, *I papi e il moderno. Una lettura del cattolicesimo contemporaneo (1903–2016)* (Brescia: Morcelliana, 2017).

the theological *ressourcement* of the papacy in Francis's style and format of teaching. In Francis's "magisterium of the daily homilies,"[10] the sources of the *ressourcement* of Vatican II—the fathers of the church—are no longer dominant as they used to be in the pontificate of Benedict XVI; Francis realigns the canon of the sources of papal teaching with a more universal and less Europe-centered cultural canon.[11] It is a re-inculturation of the papacy that relies more on the wisdom of experience as a source for theology, following the theology of Vatican II's document on revelation, *Dei Verbum*:

> This tradition which comes from the Apostles develop in the Church with the help of the Holy Spirit. For there is a growth in the understanding of the realities and the words which have been handed down. This happens through the contemplation and study made by believers, who treasure these things in their hearts (see Luke, 2:19, 51) through a penetrating understanding of the spiritual realities which they experience, and through the preaching of those who have received through Episcopal succession the sure gift of truth. For as the centuries succeed one another, the Church constantly moves forward toward the fullness of divine truth until the words of God reach their complete fulfillment in her. (*DV*, no. 8)

Francis's re-inculturation of the papacy reveals a pluralization of the forms and sources of papal teaching, not only the teaching of the gestures inaugurated by his predecessors, especially John XXIII and Paul VI, but also the rediscovery of the different dimensions of the pastoral ministry of the bishop of Rome as a priest celebrating the Eucharist with the people every day. This is a complex mix of new and old in a dynamism that Italian theologian Severino Dianich has described as the awareness

---

[10] See Severino Dianich, *Magistero in movimento. Il caso papa Francesco* (Bologna: EDB, 2015), 57–62.

[11] See Massimo Borghesi, *The Mind of Pope Francis: The Intellectual Journey of Jorge Mario Bergoglio*, trans. Barry Hudock (Collegeville, MN: Liturgical Press, 2018), in Italian, *Jorge Mario Bergoglio. Una biografia intellettuale* (Milan: Jaca Book, 2017).

in Francis that "the multiplicity of the expressions of the faith cannot be deprived of a universal grammar."[12] This re-inculturation of the papacy has found expression also in one of the most visible aspects of the contemporary papacy, that is, the foreign trips of the pope. Fifteen of the twenty-four international trips of Benedict XVI (2005–13) were in Europe. In the first six years of Francis's pontificate (2013–19), only 33 percent were to European countries, 29 percent to Asian countries, and 26 percent to countries in the Americas. He visited seventeen nations with a Catholic majority, ten with a Muslim majority, five with an Eastern Orthodox majority, and two with a Buddhist majority. Only three of the forty-five nations visited were Catholic and Western European countries (Ireland, Poland, and Portugal), and seven of the European nations he visited were historically non-Catholic countries in Europe (Albania, Bosnia-Herzegovina, Greece, Sweden, Romania, Bulgaria, and Macedonia).

This map of Francis's papal trips was the coherent execution of a decision signaled by Francis early in his pontificate. In the first address to the crowd immediately after the election, Francis spoke about himself as bishop in relation to his people. In the official *Annuario Pontificio*, published in May 2013, two months after Francis's election, there were only two lines for the description of the title of the new pope: "Francesco, vescovo di Roma"—Francis, bishop of Rome—while all his previous titles were bumped to the next page.[13]

This new emphasis on the role of bishop of Rome meant a new relationship between the local and the universal in Francis's ministry: a more visible papal ministry in the city of Rome, more present in the global world, and a different kind of relationship with Italy and Western Europe. In a time when globalization means more connections among urban giants and fewer connections with their peripheries, Francis's engagement with the Catholic churches out of Europe led to a renewed pastoral attention to the city of Rome, visible, for example, in his meeting on March 21, 2014, with Fr. Luigi Ciotti, founder of the association Libera (an association with Catholics and non-Catholics,

---

[12] Dianich, *Magistero in movimento*, 65.
[13] *Annuario Pontificio 2013* (Vatican City: Libreria Editrice Vaticana, 2013).

engaged in fighting the mafia) and known for his difficult relations with the Vatican in the past. Francis and Fr. Ciotti met in a Roman parish just a few blocks from the Vatican to pray for the victims of organized crime in a moment of both religious prayer and civil resistance.[14] Karl Rahner's famous characterization of the church of Vatican II as a world church becomes in Francis a city church, with the world seen as a city and a metropolis.[15] Francis's ecclesiology of globalization is articulated in his theology for the contemporary multicultural and multi-religious city compared to Benedict XVI's inclination for a medieval monastic theology.

The re-inculturation of the papacy also meant changes in liturgies and ceremonies that communicate the ecclesiological relationship between Rome and the local churches, such as the decision, announced on January 28, 2015, to give the pallium to new metropolitan archbishops not in Rome but in their local churches through the apostolic nuncio in a ceremony tasked to emphasize the synodality of the local churches thanks to the participation of all the bishops of the province.[16] In a similar way, Francis's decision to give back to the national bishops' conferences authority over liturgical translation, announced with the motu proprio *Magnum Principium* of September 2017, is part of an ecclesiological reorientation of the papacy related to the post–Vatican II ecclesiological debate—but it also ushered in a new phase in the two-thousand-year history of inculturation of the papacy.[17] In both cases Francis's decision is not a renunciation of the ecclesiological prerogatives of Rome but a rereading of those prerogatives in light of a new situation of the global church and a rebalancing of the attempts under John Paul II

---

[14] For Pope Francis's address on this occasion, see the Vatican website.

[15] See Karl Rahner, "Basic Theological Interpretation of the Second Vatican Council," in Karl Rahner, *Concern for the Church* (New York: Crossroad, 1981), 77–90.

[16] See Gerard O'Connell, "Pope Decides Pallium Will Be Given to Metropolitan Archbishops in Home Dioceses," *America* (January 28, 2015).

[17] For liturgy and ecclesiological decentralization, see Massimo Faggioli, *True Reform: Liturgy and Ecclesiology in* Sacrosanctum Concilium (Collegeville, MN: Liturgical Press, 2012), esp. 125–44.

and Benedict XVI to make the ecclesial peripheries procedurally and theologically more connected to the center and under its hierarchical control.

One of the typical antinomies and tensions of the culture and theology of the Jesuits is the polar tension between Catholic universality and local inculturation. In our postmodern times and for Pope Francis, the polar tension is rephrased between globalization and localization in the image of the church as a polyhedron, where the tension between local and universal is not resolved in favor of one or the other but is kept in tension.[18]

Institutional and Missionary Catholicism in the Global World

This new inculturation of the papacy is not based on a self-sufficient understanding of the church and Catholicism but is part of a new comprehension of the meaning of the catholicity of Catholicism in globalization.

The new paradigm for the relationship between Roman Catholicism and the global world is being built by making evident the deep connections among all human beings and between humans and creation. *Laudato Si'* is not just the culmination of previous papal teaching on the subject but also part of the larger picture in which the issue of the environment is part of a renewed cosmological awareness in the papal magisterium. It is not a disincarnated cosmology but part of the steps taken in acknowledging the existence of a chain of relations among all living beings as the foundation for an ecclesiology of globalization that is still in the making.[19]

---

[18] See Borghesi, *Jorge Mario Bergoglio*, 84, 132–33, 145. See also Drew Christiansen, "The Global Vision of *Evangelii Gaudium*: Cultural Diversity as a Road to Peace," in *Pope Francis and the Future of Catholicism: Evangelii Gaudium and the Papal Agenda*, ed. Gerard Mannion (New York: Cambridge University Press, 2017), 203–20.

[19] See Bryan T. Froehle and Mary L. Gautier, *Global Catholicism: Portrait of a World Church* (Maryknoll, NY: Orbis Books, 2003); Neil J. Ormerod and Shane Clifton, *Globalization and the Mission of the Church* (London: T & T Clark, 2011); Richard R. Gaillardetz,

Francis makes it clear that a Catholic theology of globalization needs to rediscover and update twentieth-century and conciliar theology that now risks being forgotten in the controversies around Vatican II. This means:

- a theology of migrations in the midst of the crisis of the nation-state;
- a theology of culture in the crisis of multiculturalism; and
- a theology of science and of knowledge in this age of global skepticism arising concurrently alongside new religious fundamentalisms.[20]

Pope Francis represents a key step in the Catholic Church's attempt to make our gaze on the world and all of humanity "a catholic gaze, in order to let our theology become truly Catholic," as Paul Zulehner writes.[21] The rethinking of the space for the church in the modern global world must be seen in the context of the rejection of the attempts to sectarianize Catholicism. In the words of one of the most important Catholic theologians, German-French Jesuit Christoph Theobald, what divides the Catholic Church today

is the concept of "catholicity": where some fear a "sectarianization" of the Catholic Church, or even its contamination by the de-institutionalization of religion and forms of evangelicalism, others see the necessary respect for its charismatic foundation which is impossible to restrict completely within the ecclesiastical institutions.[22]

Ecclesiology for a Global Church: A People Called and Sent (Maryknoll, NY: Orbis Books, 2008); and Susanna Snyder, Agnes M. Brazal, and Joshua Ralston, eds., *Church in an Age of Global Migration: A Moving Body* (New York: Palgrave Macmillan, 2016).

[20] See, for example, Roberto Calasso, *L'innominabile attuale* (Milan: Adelphi, 2017); and Pankaj Mishra, *The Age of Anger: A History of the Present* (New York: Farrar, Straus and Giroux, 2017).

[21] Paul Michael Zulehner, "Teologia della globalizzazione," *Il Regno—attualità* 9 (2015): 591.

[22] Christoph Theobald, *Urgences pastorales du moment présent. Comprendre, partager, réformer* (Paris: Bayard, 2017), 101.

Typical of Francis's ecclesiology of globalization is a particular relationship between the two foci of Catholic ecclesiology at Vatican II, the *ad intra* and the *ad extra*. Vatican II proceeded from a debate on ecclesiology *ad intra* (from the preparatory schema for the discussion of the council about the church, *De Ecclesia*, of 1960–62 to the ecclesiological debate, especially in 1963, leading to the constitution *Lumen Gentium*) to one on an ecclesiology *ad extra* (the constitution *Gaudium et Spes*, the last document approved by the council on the last day, December 7, 1965). Francis is indeed proceeding in a different direction: renewing the *ad intra* through the insertion of the *ad extra* in the theological-magisterial discourse and the ecclesial experience of the Catholic Church: "With Vatican II, the church has found a new self-understanding as a world church, both in the sense of a church in the diversity of cultures and in the sense of a church that is always understood and implemented looking at it from the world and culture. . . . The church no longer understands itself 'in relation' to the world, but as a church 'in' the world."[23]

This new Catholic global vision is also geopolitical and historical-philosophical. Francis's pontificate must be seen as another stage in the history of Catholicism taking stock of the end of the Christian empires, which with the election of Francis was embodied by the first non-European pope. This was announced already by Cardinal Bergoglio's speech in the pre-conclave, with his emphasis on the peripheries, which was "a response against the challenges of globalization, while Benedict XVI was more preoccupied with the future of Christianity in Europe."[24] Francis embodies a post-European Catholic sense of the universality of the church, with a clear sense of the meaning of the irruption of America (in the sense of Latin

---

[23] Margit Eckholt, *An die Peripherie gehen. In der Spuren des armen Jesus. Vom Zweiten Vatikanum zu Papst Franziskus* (Ostfildern: Grünewald, 2015), 57.

[24] Giovanni Vian, "Le Pape François et la mondialisation. Un pontificat pour un christianisme global?" in *Le pontificat romaine dans l'epoque contemporaine*, ed. Giovanni Vian, 231–35 (Venice: Università Ca' Foscari, 2018), 220.

America) in history.[25] The irruption of America signified by the Latin America of Pope Francis means not only the end of the Spanish colonial empire, but also of the other European empires, namely, the British. This irruption of America means a new protagonism of the *pueblo*.[26] The relationship between the *ad intra* and *ad extra* in contemporary Catholicism has both a geopolitical and a geocultural dimension.

Also typical of Francis's pontificate is the intimate connection between Catholic ecclesiology and an internationalist view of globalization that refuses to shrink Catholicism to an identity-driven religious community with a geopolitical center housed in the West. Indubitably, John Paul II put the Catholic Church firmly in the Western camp during the Cold War; after the end of the Cold War, John Paul II made some adjustments (that went largely unnoticed in the United States), especially about social and economic justice, toward a more critical stance toward capitalism. Benedict XVI reasserted the European and Western alignment of the Catholic Church and made this entrenchment more binding theologically and culturally.[27] After the shock of 9/11 and the newly visible crisis in the West, Benedict XVI repeatedly made clear the need for a theological and geopolitical connection between Catholicism and the West. His statements (both before and after his election to the papacy) on Islam as a theological-political problem were part of this connection.

Francis has put this alignment into question, to say the least. Benedict XVI was the first pope elected in the post–9/11 world. But for Jorge Mario Bergoglio the event of 9/11—and the Synod of Bishops taking in place in Rome immediately after the attacks

---

[25] *La irrupción de América en la historia* is the title of one of the books of Argentinian philosopher Amelia Podetti, one of the most important intellectuals in Bergoglio's intellectual biography (see Borghesi, *Jorge Mario Bergoglio*, 56–57, 165).

[26] Borghesi, *Jorge Mario Bergoglio*, 53.

[27] See Benedict XVI's lecture at the University of Regensburg, September 12, 2006, titled "Faith, Reason and the University: Memories and Reflections"; and Benedict XVI, *Address to the German Parliament* (September 22, 2011).

against the United States—mark the ascent of the future pope to the global stage of Catholicism, when Archbishop Jorge Mario Bergoglio was called to substitute, in his role of general relator at the Synod of Bishops in Rome on the ministry of the bishops, for the archbishop of New York, Cardinal Edward Michael Egan, who could not reach Rome in the aftermath of the terrorist attacks. September 2001 was a collision of the church with globalization, but also the access to the stage of global Catholicity for the future Pope Francis.[28]

Both Benedict and Francis had to face multifaceted challenges: *globalization* for the Catholic institution and imagination in terms of multiculturalism; a *political and economic anti-globalization* movement in the form of ethno-nationalism and religious traditionalism and fundamentalism; and a *cultural and theological localism* that rejects bonds of solidarity and of mutual obedience in the church and in secular and pluralistic society. The question of the boundaries of the church, of "who belongs to the church," is being reframed by the global Catholic Church at a time when the question of another "natural" kind of belonging, to the nation or the state or the people in ethnic and racial terms, tends to be framed in exclusionary terms. In this there is a continuity in the magisterial tradition of all the popes, at least since Vatican II.

The responses of the last two popes to those global changes have been significantly different. Francis is the pope whose pontificate has seen the crisis of globalization and also of the culture of Catholic internationalism, as well as the limits of the reformability and governability of the institutional Catholic Church.[29] We must see Francis's ecclesiology of globalization in this framework. He has shaped his pontificate in an effort to link the issue of the sustainability of the *institutional dimension* of the Catholic Church with a *post-institutional missionary effort* of the church in the global world. Typical of his approach is the important speech he gave to the Congregation for Bishops on

---

[28] See Iacopo Scaramuzzi, *Tango Vaticano. La Chiesa al tempo di Francesco* (Rome: Edizioni dell'Asino, 2015), 35, 81–86.

[29] See Giorgio Agamben, *The Mystery of Evil: Benedict XVI and the End of Days* (Stanford, CA: Stanford University Press, 2017), original in Italian (Rome-Bari: Laterza, 2013).

February 27, 2014, about the model of bishop and the pastorality of the church: "The episcopate does not exist for itself but for the Church, for the flock, for others, especially for those whom the world would throw away." The creation of the new Dicastery for Promoting Integral Human Development, in August 2016, was another element in the institutional expression of the global consciousness of Pope Francis. The statutes of the new dicastery could be read as a summary of Francis's priorities for the sociopolitical message of the church:

> The Dicastery also expresses the Holy Father's care for suffering humanity, including the needy, the sick and the excluded, and pays special attention to the needs and issues of those who are forced to flee their homeland, the stateless, the marginalized, victims of armed conflicts and natural disasters, the imprisoned, the unemployed, victims of contemporary forms of slavery and torture, and others whose dignity is endangered. . . . In fulfilling its mission, the Dicastery may establish relationships with associations, institutes and non-governmental organizations, including those outside the Catholic Church, who are committed to promoting justice and peace. It may also enter into discussion with representatives of civil governments and other international public institutions, in order to promote study, deepen knowledge, and public awareness regarding matters within its competence, while respecting the competencies of other offices of the Roman Curia.[30]

This global approach means not only a new composition of the global leadership of the Catholic Church, visible, for example, in the profile of bishops appointed by Francis and in creating more cardinals from the global south and from non-Catholic majority countries in the College of Cardinals.[31] It means also challenging traditional ways of dividing different portions of global Catholicism in different juridical situations that make

---

[30] Francis, *Statutes of the Dicastery for Promoting Integral Human Development*, August 17, 2016.

[31] For up-to-date information on the College of Cardinals, see the dedicated page of the Holy See Press Office on the Vatican website.

little sense pastorally and from a missionary point of view today. For example, in June 2014, Cardinal Sandri, the prefect of the Congregation for the Oriental Churches, published a decree allowing Eastern Catholic bishops in the diaspora to ordain married men, thereby revising a previous decree that had been in place since 1929. In October 2017, Pope Francis created the necessary structures so that Syro-Malabar and Syro-Malankara Christians moving to places outside Kerala (India) would no longer be pastorally dependent upon the Latin-rite bishops.

Ecclesial and Ecclesiological Responses to Globalization

The responses of Francis's church to globalization are not only in terms of institutional structure, communication strategy, and political alignments, but also, and primarily, in theological and ecclesiological terms. In a time when the political responses to globalization are often shaped by the politics of fear, Francis understands the challenge to the church from this kind of reaction against globalization; fear is not only a formidable challenge against a Christian worldview,[32] but also a powerful agent of de-solidarization/against solidarity.[33] Further, fear is rooted in a lost sense of space in this age of global migrations and also the nomadism of non-migrants.

The most important theological response elaborated by Francis in this time of crisis has been the determination to reject in the strongest possible terms the temptation of a retreat, of an option for self-defense by Catholicism—ecclesial or ecclesiastical, institutional, communitarian, cultural, or spiritual. The rejection of the option of retreat is part of Francis's view of the call to holiness expressed in the exhortation *Gaudete et Exsultate* (2018). His view of holiness is not individual but ecclesial in the sense of a collective effort in the midst of the people: "Not infrequently, contrary to the promptings of the Spirit, the life of the church can become a museum piece or the possession of a select few.

---

[32] See Marilynne Robinson, "Fear," in *The Givenness of Things: Essays* (New York: Farrar, Straus and Giroux, 2015), 125–40.

[33] See Zulehner, "Teologia della globalizzazione," 592.

This can occur when some groups of Christians give excessive importance to certain rules, customs or ways of acting" (no. 58). The articulation of the ecclesial and ecclesiological response of the pontificate to globalization became an icon of this papacy during the first trip outside Rome, to the island of Lampedusa on July 8, 2013, where Francis denounced the "globalization of indifference." During the homily, he said:

> In this globalized world, we have fallen into globalized indifference. We have become used to the suffering of others: it doesn't affect me; it doesn't concern me; it's none of my business! . . . The globalization of indifference makes us all "unnamed," responsible, yet nameless and faceless.

The consequences have been not in terms of ritualized denunciation, but of a call to ecclesiological and theological transformation: this has amounted to a challenge for the political-cultural appropriations of Catholic orthodoxy by some Catholic milieus in the Northern Atlantic hemisphere. It is what Clemens Sedmak has called the "transformation of orthodoxy" under Pope Francis: "We are pilgrims in the middle of a journey. Propositional orthodoxy opens new doors for moral and doctrinal temptations, such as the moral temptation of self-righteousness and the doctrinal temptation to see revelation as a possession that can be fully controlled."[34]

Francis's emphasis on the "church for the poor" must be understood not as an endorsement of liberation theology from the first Latin American pope, but rather as a moment that begins before liberation theology and goes beyond liberation theology. Francis reclaims one of the most overlooked passages of the Second Vatican Council: "Just as Christ carried out the work of redemption in poverty and persecution, so the church is called to follow the same route that it might communicate the fruits of salvation to men" (*LG*, no. 8). Francis does not quote it directly, but his ecclesiology expresses an institutional exegesis of this passage that no other pope of the post–Vatican II period

---

[34] Clemens Sedmak, *A Church of the Poor: Pope Francis and the Transformation of Orthodoxy* (Maryknoll, NY: Orbis Books, 2016), 169.

has had the courage to express about the church and poverty.[35] This new approach to the issue of the church and poverty had effects in different Catholic churches, including his own Latin America: "Pope Francis has since the 1980s 'rehabilitated' the theology of liberation and his pontificate has contributed to the de-ideologization of the theological debate in Latin America."[36] De-ideologization of Catholic teaching goes together with a new role for the peripheries of the church. The emphasis on *the peripheries* is another example of this pontificate's response to globalization, which is pushing the church into a profound change in the relationship with its ideological ally, the Western world. Globalization is also revealing a reversal of roles between Catholicism and its major ideological enemy in the twentieth century, Marxism. The peripheries, which were once the cradle of hope for those who believed in the socialist and communist project, have been gradually abandoned by liberal-progressive political ideologies and have now become a major focus of the papacy. The new social and economic relations between centers and peripheries from the twentieth century to the twenty-first century have also changed the geography of hope. Francis's project is not about decentralizing church structures, but about bringing lived Christianity back to the peripheries "as a starting point to develop a new intelligence of our reality."[37] This is the backdrop of his November 13, 2015, meeting[38] with the theologians gathering in Rome for the fiftieth anniversary of the "Catacomb Pact" signed at the end of Vatican II, in 1965, and, almost fifty years later, the message Francis sent to the thirteenth meeting of the basic ecclesial communities in Brazil of January 2014, the first message of a pope to the basic ecclesial

---

[35] See Corrado Lorefice, *Dossetti e Lercaro. La Chiesa povera e dei poveri nella prospettiva del Concilio Vaticano II* (Milan: Paoline, 2011). Lorefice was appointed archbishop of Palermo (Italy) by Francis in December 2015.

[36] Eckholt, *An die Peripherie gehen*, 108.

[37] See Andrea Riccardi, *Periferie. Crisi e novità per la Chiesa* (Milan: Jaca Book, 2016), 119; in English, *To the Margins: Pope Francis and the Mission of the Church* (Maryknoll, NY: Orbis Books, 2018).

[38] See "Papst begrüßt Befreiungstheologen," a report of the meeting in German, at Radio Vatikan, November 13, 2015, http://de.radiovaticana.va/news/2015/11/13/papst_begrüßt_befreiungstheologen/1186548.

communities after decades of tense relationship between the papal magisterium and that experience of church typical of Latin America.[39] The ecclesiological paradigm shift of Francis is a *historical-geographical* shift in the context of the globalization crisis. It is an *historical-theological* shift from an understanding of mission and evangelization that at Vatican II was still conceived in geographical-spatial terms to a relational and cultural response to the crisis of Catholic geopolitics; this is the thrust of the conciliar decree *Ad Gentes* in Francis's pontificate.[40] Francis's ecclesiological response to the crisis of globalization and to the new Catholic globalization is also a shift in the missionary responsibility from the *institutional* church—bishops and clergy as presiders of local geographical communities—to a responsibility of the *charismatic* and *pneumatological* structure of the church in evangelization.[41] In the tension between different poles and pulls, Francis balances the institutional and spatial dimensions of the church with a mystical, trans-border dimension. Francis continues on the trajectory of Vatican II, which initiated the process of disentangling catholicity from its geographical and geopolitical understanding—a movement toward overcoming the Tridentine idea of catholicity as a homogeneous juridical space.[42] Francis is a new step in the continuing spatial and geographical "un-limitation" of catholicity.[43]

This Catholic understanding of globalization opens the space for a new prophetic voice of the church, which takes place also through a reshaping of the ecclesial and ecclesiastical spaces in favor of a church structure that is not just less institutional. It is also articulating in a different way the relations between lay and clergy, but also between secular clergy, religious orders, ecclesial movements, and the wide variety of different ways

---

[39] See Francis, "Message of Pope Francis to Participants in the 13th Meeting of the Basic Ecclesial Communities in Brazil," December 17, 2013. The meeting was held January 7–11, 2014.

[40] See Christoph Theobald, *Fraternità. Il nuovo stile della Chiesa secondo papa Francesco* (Bose: Qiqajon, 2016), 29–30.

[41] Ibid., 47.

[42] See Theobald, *Urgences pastorales du moment présent*, 105–7.

[43] See Eckholt, *An die Peripherie gehen*, 40.

of living the Christian vocation in the secular age and in the global world.[44] Francis does not believe that the function of the parish is over: "The parish is not an outdated institution; precisely because it possesses great flexibility, it can assume quite different contours depending on the openness and missionary creativity of the pastor and the community" (*EG*, no. 28). But Francis is clearly keen on overcoming the excessive "parishization" typical of Catholicism after the Council of Trent[45] and what has been called the "parish civilization."[46] This is the context of Francis's emphasis on sanctuaries, on social and ecclesial movements, and on the peripheries, all of which express a concept of space in the church that is a response to the crisis of the ecclesiastical *ancien regime*, but also to the redefinition of spaces in the new architecture of visible and invisible power in the globalized world.

This also entails a departure in Catholic ecclesiology from the post–Vatican I, twentieth-century unilateral relationship between church and society. Francis's ecclesiology is based on an idea of "fraternity that is never guaranteed, always threatened by violence, and to be rebuilt once again every time."[47]

Fraternity of the church with the world commits the church to a different way of expressing brotherhood and sisterhood in the church. There is a profound relationship between this ecclesiological response to globalization and Francis's articulation of collegiality and synodality in an ecumenical context.[48] The speech of October 17, 2015, for the fiftieth anniversary of the institution of the Synod of Bishops, offered Francis a chance to develop Paul VI's intuition and to overcome its limits:

---

[44] See Massimo Faggioli, *Sorting Out Catholicism: Brief History of the New Ecclesial Movements* (Collegeville, MN: Liturgical Press, 2014).

[45] See John W. O'Malley, "Priesthood, Ministry, and Religious Life: Some Historical and Historiographical Considerations," *Theological Studies* 49 (1988): 223–57.

[46] Theobald, *Urgences pastorales du moment présent*, 99.

[47] Theobald, *Fraternità*, 82.

[48] See Hyacinte Destivelle, *Conduis-la vers l'unité parfait: oecuménisme et synodalité* (Paris: Cerf, 2018).

A synodal Church is a Church which listens, which realizes that listening "is more than simply hearing." It is a mutual listening in which everyone has something to learn. The faithful people, the college of bishops, the Bishop of Rome: all listening to each other, and all listening to the Holy Spirit, the "Spirit of truth" (*Jn* 14:17), in order to know what he "says to the Churches" (*Rev* 2:7). The Synod of Bishops is the point of convergence of this listening process conducted at every level of the Church's life. The Synod process begins by listening to the people of God, which "shares also in Christ's prophetic office," according to a principle dear to the Church of the first millennium: "*Quod omnes tangit ab omnibus tractari debet* [What touches all must be approved by all]."

The most impressive element of Francis's *magna carta* of synodality was not the elucidation of the three levels of synodality (local, middle, universal)—something ecclesiologists have developed at least since Vatican II. Most telling was the link he explicated between synodality and the church's message in the world:

Our gaze also extends to humanity as a whole. A synodal church is like a standard lifted up among the nations (cf. *Is* 11:12) in a world which—while calling for participation, solidarity and transparency in public administration—often consigns the fate of entire peoples to the grasp of small but powerful groups. As a church which "journeys together" with men and women, sharing the travails of history, let us cherish the dream that a rediscovery of the inviolable dignity of peoples and of the function of authority as service will also be able to help civil society to be built up in justice and fraternity, and thus bring about a more beautiful and humane world for coming generations.

Francis elaborates "a theology of ecclesial brotherhood and sisterhood": A poor church is "the guarantee for the church that its livelihood is the Gospel and not some other psychological resource. Mercy is the link of ecclesial brotherhood and sisterhood with the larger brotherhood and sisterhood with the whole world."[49] The ecclesiology of mercy is an ecclesiological continuation of the globalization of Catholicism of Vatican II, and at the same time a response to the crisis of globalization that does not become a return to the anti-liberal Catholic tropes of the late nineteenth and twentieth centuries.[50] The multiform ecumenism of Francis—from the patriarch of Constantinople Bartholomew of the Eastern Orthodox churches to Rabbi Abraham Skorka to the Sheikh Ahmed el-Tayeb, the grand imam of Al-Azhar, to the non-mainstream Pentecostal pastor in the little community near Naples, Giovanni Traettino—redefines boundaries that are theological as well as geopolitical.[51]

One prime example of Francis's ecclesiology of globalization and of its complex mix of theological, political, and spiritual insights was his trip to Abu Dhabi of February 2019. There was the interreligious dimension, with the Abu Dhabi statement rejecting the "political manipulation of religions" and marking a new stage in the relations between the Catholic Church and Islam.[52] There was the geopolitical dimension, with the first trip of a pope to the Arabian Peninsula being the eight-hundredth anniversary of the meeting between Francis of Assisi and the sultan in Egypt. But most of all, there was Francis's intent to give greater visibility to the significant Catholic population in the United Arab Emirates (UAE)—close to one million—almost all of them migrant laborers from Asia. In planning his papal visits Francis has always given special attention to countries where Catholics and Christians are a small minority. On the Arabian Peninsula, Roman Catholics live as a minority in the cradle of Islam. They are also a minority within a minority:

---

[49] In Giuseppe Ruggieri, *Chiesa sinodale* (Rome-Bari: Laterza, 2017), 170–71.

[50] For the ecclesiology of mercy, see Stella Morra, *Dio non si stanca. La Misericordia come forma ecclesiale* (Bologna: EDB, 2015).

[51] See Scaramuzzi, *Tango Vaticano*, 102.

[52] See "A Document for Human Fraternity for World Peace and Living Together," signed in Abu Dhabi on February 4, 2019, by Pope Francis and Grand Imam Ahmed el-Tayeb of Al-Azhar. Available on the Vatican website.

Catholics of the Roman rite are just one of the many ancient Christian communities. Francis's trip to the UAE in February 2019 served to highlight the diversity of Christian traditions in the Middle East, some of which go back to the first centuries of the church. Ecclesiology of globalization relies on *ressourcement* in the sense of a profound understanding of the historical complexity of the relations between Roman Catholicism and the Catholic minorities in Asia and Africa—an element that is often missing from the ideological reconstructions of Catholicism as a Western church. In Abu Dhabi the pope gathered the Catholic Church in its universality, in a stadium, to celebrate the Eucharist, and to acknowledge and encourage a group of Christians living in extremely difficult conditions, a group politically neglected, culturally ignored, and all but invisible to many of their coreligionists in the West. Like the "Document on Human Fraternity for World Peace and Living Together," February 4, 2019, the stadium mass showed how different the intra-Catholic debate about liberalism looks when seen through the eyes of Catholic minorities living in Muslim countries. For them, liberty is a scarce treasure rather than an outmoded abstraction. That minority Catholic church in that particular situation also deals with the issue of clericalism and the lay component of the church in ways that defy the dominant, twentieth-century perception of the partition between laity and clergy in contemporary global Catholicism.

Ecclesiology of the Laity in the Global Church

The frequent criticisms of clericalism in Francis have to do with the comprehension of the impact of globalized culture and religion on the religious self. As the pope said at a meeting with priests, religious, consecrated, and seminarians in Santiago, Chile, on January 16, 2018, "Where vocation is concerned, there is no such thing as a selfie. Vocation demands that others take your picture." Pope Francis elaborates a spiritual theology for the church of today in the context of globalization and in response to globalization. One of the main themes of his spiritual theology for a church in globalization is the theme of identity and the self. This has consequences for his vision of the church: clergy, family, and laity. The laity is part of globalization in a way that the clergy is not. One aspect that reflects the encounter between Catholic teaching and globalization is the ecclesiology of the family. Francis continued a magisterial reflection that is a fruit of the twentieth century and specifically of the Second Vatican Council and of the post–Vatican II period. In the words of Pierangelo Sequeri, appointed by Francis in August 2016 to be president of the Pontifical John Paul II Institute for Studies on Marriage and Family at the Lateran University in Rome:

> The deepening of the theology of marriage, in terms of Christian anthropology and ecclesial form, is a relatively new theme. Only for a few decades now has the doctrine of the Christian sacrament definitively surpassed its substantial confinement—in terms of method and content—within the inventory of themes of canonistic and moral interest, restoring the autonomy and breadth necessary for the intelligence of the mystery inscribed in the human and ecclesial event of the conjugal alliance.[53]

In Francis this recent attention to the ecclesiology of the family took a turn with the synods on the family of 2014 and 2015 and the post-synodal exhortation *Amoris Laetitia* in 2016, not in acceptance of the Western individualistic liberal paradigm, but in response to an absolutizing of the self that has consequences not only for individuals, but for the church as well. Catholicism is called to understand the link between "the pseudo-secular affirmation of the monotheism of the self and pseudo-religious foundation of the annihilation of the other."[54] Francis's careful emphasis on his ecclesiology of the family demonstrates the distance between Francis and Western liberalism, and thus how misguided it is to identify Francis simply as a liberal Catholic.

---

[53] Pierangelo Sequeri, "Il grembo famigliare dell'amore Chiesa e famiglia nell'*Amoris Laetitia*," in *La Rivista del Clero Italiano* 1 (2017): 7.

[54] Pierangelo Sequeri, *La cruna dell'ego. Uscire dal monoteismo del sé* (Milan: Vita e Pensiero, 2017), 12.

But what reveals more about the ecclesial and ecclesiological responses of Francis's church to globalization is his ecclesiology of the laity; that is, the changes it advises in the role of the church in the world and of the laity in the church. Francis's ecclesiology is based on the theology of the laity developed since the 1950s by the most important theologian of Vatican II, Yves Congar.[55] But it is also based on one of the great intuitions of Congar about ecclesiology and reform: pastoral primacy, the need for all priests-theologians to stay involved in pastoral ministry[56] and, in the church of today, for all lay theologians to become involved in pastoral ministry. This was one of the early insights of the young Bergoglio in 1976 as rector of a college: "Following this theology, the second point of the Bergoglio reform called for the students at the [Colegio] Máximo to go into the neighborhoods to play with the children, to teach the catechism, and to understand better the problems faced by the families there."[57] Francis's ecclesiology of globalization comes from the new relationship created between the clergy and the families of the neighborhood surrounding the Colegio Máximo in Buenos Aires almost forty years before his election to the papacy.

On the other hand, Francis does not have the type of ecclesiology of the laity—a theology of the *quid est laicus?* (what is a lay person?)—that emphasizes the supposedly ontological difference between the ordained and the rest of the church. Francis talks often about the laity, mostly by addressing the problem of clericalism. The most important document of the pontificate on the laity thus far is the letter he addressed to the president of the Pontifical Commission for America Latina, Cardinal Ouellet, on March 19, 2016. He writes:

Looking at the People of God is remembering that we all enter the Church as lay people. The first sacrament, which

---

[55] See Christopher Bellitto, "True and False Reform: Francis's Middle Way," *The Tablet*, January 3, 2015.

[56] See Yves Congar, *True and False Reform in the Church* (Collegeville, MN: Liturgical Press, 2010), 218–22.

[57] Borghesi, *The Mind of Pope Francis*, 45.

seals our identity forever, and of which we should always be proud, is Baptism. Through Baptism and by the anointing of the Holy Spirit, (the faithful) "are consecrated as a spiritual house and a holy priesthood" (*Lumen Gentium*, n. 10). Our first and fundamental consecration is rooted in our Baptism. No one has been baptized a priest or a bishop. They baptized us as lay people and it is the indelible sign that no one can ever erase. It does us good to remember that the Church is not an elite of priests, of consecrated men, of bishops, but that everyone forms the faithful Holy People of God.

Francis has addressed nonritual messages to the new ecclesial lay movements, inviting them not to see themselves as elites in the church, but as servants of the ecclesial communion;[58] however, he does not talk often about the laity as a distinct part of the church, in contrast to John Paul II and Benedict XVI.

Francis's view of the laity in the church stems from his ecclesiology of the people,[59] which reflects an ecclesiological thinking that is more horizontal than the traditionally vertical, multilayered Catholic ecclesiology. The fact that the most important Synod of Bishops celebrated under Francis was about family and marriage—typically a lay theme—is evidence of his awareness of the need to embark upon synodality from a non-clerical sphere of ecclesial life. In the global church, with different cultures of marriage and family, Francis reopened an ecclesial process aimed at a theological reflection that traditionally has seen the laity on the receiving end of the discussion. Peter Brown, the great historian of Christian late antiquity, spoke about the debate on marriage in the fifth century between Augustine and Julian of Eclanus: "This was the last great debate in the Latin West, between the fifth century and the Reformation, to be conducted before an audience that included influential and cultivated mar-

---

[58] See Massimo Faggioli, *The Rising Laity: Ecclesial Movements since Vatican II* (Mahwah, NJ: Paulist Press, 2016), 131–53.

[59] See Rafael Luciani, *El papa Francisco y la teología del pueblo* (Madrid: PPC, 2016), in English, *Pope Francis and the Theology of the People* (Maryknoll, NY: Orbis Books, 2017).

ried persons on issues (such as sex and marriage) that directly touched their lives."[60] The pastorality of church teaching on family and marriage today has to do with the new globalized laity. In today's globalized church the distinction between the laity and clergy no longer works through the reception or exportation of cultural and symbolic aggregates of European origin, but crosses different junctions from the past that have to do with many elements, including the new missionary and ministeriality of the church in the secularized world, and a new relationship with the secular and the temporal.[61] In response to the crisis of parallelism and isomorphism of church and state,[62] a new laity has emerged that is affected by the fracture of the social covenant that involves the church. It is a laity

- broken along social and economic lines, in a situation of increasing socioeconomic inequalities;
- broken along ethnic lines, a Catholicism that immigrates but struggles to mingle and tends to reproduce often in national or linguistic parishes;
- broken along national lines, in the context of resurging nationalisms against the internationalism of Pope Francis; and
- broken along fractured ideological-political fault lines in an expansion to the globe of the American "culture wars."

All these dimensions touch the laity more than the clergy in the global church, and this is where Francis's rediscovery of the Aristotelian *zoon politikon* (political animal), since *Evangelii Gaudium*, finds significant obstacles: in the fragmentation of the

---

[60] Peter Brown, *Through the Eye of a Needle: Wealth, the Fall of Rome, and the Making of Christianity in the West, 350–550 AD* (Princeton, NJ: Princeton University Press, 2012), 376.

[61] See Charles Taylor, *A Secular Age* (Cambridge, MA: Belknap Press of Harvard University Press, 2007).

[62] See Paolo Prodi, "Europe in the Age of Reformations: The Modern State and Confessionalization," *Catholic Historical Review* 103, no. 1 (Winter 2017): 1–19, in Italian, "Senza Stato né Chiesa. L'Europa a cinquecento anni dalla Riforma," *Il Mulino* 1 (2017): 7–23.

ecclesial body.[63] The laity as such is no longer identifiable in one kind of lay Catholic. It is a laity also divided by the question of gender and the question of the role of women in the church. The Catholic global laity is a fragmented laity without unifying organizations or initials or slogans as in the twentieth century; it is not unified by the political parties that unite the Catholic Western laity. We are at the end of the Catholic melting pot represented by the Catholic Action and the Christian democratic parties in the twentieth century of the Second Vatican Council (in Europe) and by the once-natural confluence of Catholicism with a political party (like the Democratic Party in the United States until the 1970s).

The pontificate of Francis meets a new phase in the acceleration of the de-Europeanization and de-Westernization of Catholicism, which also means a redefinition of the relations between the laity as a theological and canon law category, on one hand, and as identification with a social, economic, and political block, on the other hand. The global Catholic laity is now going through, with a couple of generations of delay, the path traveled by the episcopate at the time of Vatican II. Catholic ecclesiology in the twentieth century and at Vatican II faced the challenge of redefining the episcopate *outside*, if not *against* the traditional (for continental Europe) identification of the episcopate with the aristocracy—a social and political identification that was based not on the small percentage of aristocrats who were recruited in the Catholic episcopal body, but on the whole church system in Catholic Europe. The slow end of the dominance of aristocracy in the church meant also a redefinition of the relationship between the Catholic Church and the land—in light of the importance of land ownership for the definition of aristocracy.[64]

The same is happening today for the laity. The global Catholic laity no longer identifies with the social stratum of European extraction that stood between proletariat and middle-class bourgeoisie. The new accents of Francis's teaching on marriage and

---

[63] See Paolo Boschini, "Il ritorno dello *zoon politikon*. L'antropologia politica di *Evangelii Gaudium*," *Rivista di Teologia dell'Evangelizzazione* 22, no. 44 (July–December 2018): 335–55.

[64] See Karl Ferdinand Werner, *Naissance de la noblesse: l'essor des élites politiques en Europe*, 2nd ed. (Paris: Fayard, 1998).

family are the result of changes not only in the sociology of the global Catholic laity, which has always been different from the European idealization of the laity, but also the result of a new relevance of the Catholic laity of Catholicism in the global south beyond the Euro–North Atlantic bourgeois ideal and the moralism linked to that ideal. Here *Gaudium et Spes* plays a particular role: "From the perspective of the south of the world, *Gaudium et Spes* is the decisive Vatican II document, which led toward a new spelling out of the catholicity of the church—one of the 'notae ecclesiae.'"[65]

It is a laity in which the walls of the "Catholic ghetto" were razed and then dispersed into the multicultural and multireligious global society, especially in the West. But it is also a laity in which the theologically traditionalist and politically and culturally identitarian impulses reemerged in the last decade in order to push fringes of the ideologized laity into "intentional communities" committed to a withdrawal from a sociality lived in common with the rest of humanity and of the church. The recent North American debate about the option of withdrawing militant Christianity from the public sphere following the defeats suffered in the "culture wars"—the so-called Benedict option and its variations[66]—is an almost exclusively lay debate; the clerical and episcopal appendices do not define its profile.

It is no coincidence that it is a debate carried out largely by recent converts who have chosen Catholicism as an ideological refuge from secularization and from theological and political liberalism. It is not only the quest for a new ecclesial imagination, but also for new *habitats* in terms of separate ecclesial and Christian spaces. Like radical orthodoxy, this quest for new ecclesial habitats is a theology made by lay people, who imagine a postmodern neo-medievalism and reject the idea of a Catholic laity immersed in a secularized world, thus rejecting the twentieth-century emphasis on political and social obligations. It is a laity that has abandoned a style of militancy: it is no

---

[65] Eckholt, *An die Peripherie gehen*, 44.

[66] See Rod Dreher, *The Benedict Option: A Strategy for Christians in a Post-Christian Nation* (New York: Sentinel, 2017). Dreher here develops from his *Crunchy Cons: The New Conservative Counterculture and Its Return to Roots* (New York: Three Rivers Press, 2006), chap. 8.

longer mobilized, because the concept of mobilization itself has entered a crisis in Western society. The crisis in the mobilization of the Catholic laity is part of the crisis of democracies, in and beyond Europe.

In the nineteenth century, Catholicism, having lost the hope of a recovery of temporal power, launched a retreat from the *imperium* (political, state power of the church) to the *sacerdotium* (the religious power), which implied a further step in the submission of the laity to the clergy. The twentieth century saw the turning point of the theology of the laity and of the common priesthood of the laity, but that turning point did not correspond to any actual change in the clerical system. At the same time, the twentieth century made possible the great development of Catholic movements that changed the connotations of Catholicism, especially the face of the laity.

The twenty-first century sees a Catholic Church in which the lines between lay identity and clerical identity are much less defined compared to only a few decades ago. This blurring of the lines that mark the distinction between clergy and laity is part of the experience of many lay Catholics, and it is also part of the reason for the reaction of part of the clergy in favor of a new phase of underscoring the boundaries and the distance between clergy and laity.

The message of Francis continues in the wake of twentieth-century Catholic conciliar ecclesiology, overcoming not only the ecclesiology of the *duo genera christianorum* (there are two different kinds of Christians: lay and ordained) but also the ecclesiology of the *duo genera laicorum* (there are two kinds of lay Catholics: the members of Catholic movements and the others). Francis has dismissed the idea of a superiority of the organized and ideologically mobilized laity as the perfect model of a healthy laity, superior to the indistinct laity within the ecclesial communion. The vision of a missionary mobilization of the whole church redefines the symbolic and organizational distinction between clergy and laity, and also within the laity. This has consequences also for the central government of the Catholic Church and is thus one of the major tests for any pontificate. This part of the papal office is also being reframed in light of the vision of a global Catholicity.

5

Global Governance
of the Catholic Church

Ours is the age of a crisis of trust in institutions and a crisis of
governance of institutions at all levels—local, national, international, and global. The Catholic Church is a multi-secular
organization, one of the oldest institutions in the world with an
uninterrupted tradition of centralized administration over vast
territories and numerous and diverse peoples over the centuries.
But the Catholic Church also is going through a crisis in its
stability and governance. The election of Francis was in part an
attempt to stabilize the papacy after the crisis in the governance
of the Vatican by Benedict XVI.

Italian historian Andrea Riccardi sums up the contribution of
Francis to the current crisis of governance:

> Bergoglio has a deep sense of institutions. . . . He does not
> come from a reality foreign to Church government, he is
> not a hermit or an intellectual, but he was provincial of the
> Jesuits, auxiliary and coadjutor bishop, and archbishop of
> a big archdiocese. He has familiarity with the government
> of the Catholic Church, but he knows that the Church is
> not made by its leaders and institutions.[1]

---

[1] Andrea Riccardi, *La sorpresa di papa Francesco. Crisi e futuro
della Chiesa* (Milan: Mondadori, 2013), 168.

Francis's pontificate seems to be a rebalancing after two pontificates of charismatic popes (each in his own way) who were largely uninterested in governing the global church. The pope given to the church by the conclave of 2013 has proven to be a surprise also for the issue of church governance. The cardinals who elected Francis expected institutional stabilization rather than the theological and spiritual path of radical renewal opened by his pontificate. This was not only the expectation of many cardinals, but also of many Catholics. Francis was elected in a conclave shaped by the hope for a restoration of the institutional stability of the Catholic Church, and of the central government of the church in the Vatican especially, in an unprecedented situation: the coexistence of the pope who was newly elected by the conclave of 2013 and the pope who had just resigned, Pope Benedict XVI, who has cohabited the Vatican with his successor in the years since his resignation.

One of the assumptions of Francis's election in March 2013 was the succession to the theologian-pope Benedict XVI with a pope of institutional stabilization, Francis. It is not clear if and how the succession from Benedict to Francis corresponded to this expectation. During the pontificate of Francis it has become more and more visible and clear that the "Catholic question" centers around the sustainability of the church in the face of a growing crisis regarding the authority and credibility of the ecclesiastical institution. But it also has become clear that examining the role of the church and its governability was growing increasingly important in the context of a crisis of systems in the crisis of globalization; the crisis of the church/churches is just another aspect of the crisis of politics and of the nation-state and of the world order in the Western world.[2] Still, political developments in many countries in the world—beginning with the United States and the European Union—made many look at the Vatican and the Catholic Church as an island of relative institutional stability in a world in a state of chaos.

In this sense the perennial question of the *ecclesia semper reformanda*—of a church that needs to be governed and at the same time constantly needs to reform itself—changes in the

---

[2] See Massimo Faggioli, *Pope Francis: Tradition in Transition* (Mahwah, NJ: Paulist Press, 2015), 41–60.

global context of the twenty-first century. It is a different urgency from the Catholic Church of Paul VI or John Paul II, for the face of the Catholic Church takes different shapes in light of different historical-political situations, both nationally and globally. Francis's pontificate has had to face a double challenge: governing a church in a world in geopolitical turmoil dealing with the disruption of globalization,[3] and governing a church internally more complex, divided, diverse, post-confessional, and trans-confessional than ever before.

The pontificate of Francis has not provided a definitive answer to the question of the possibilities for reforming and governing the institutions of the Catholic Church: certainly Francis has rediscovered the language of collegiality, synodality, a new relationship between universal and local church, and a rereading of the papacy formulated by Vatican I in a long-term history of ecclesiology.[4] The reversal of expectations between the conclave and the pontificate of Francis has changed the position of the pontificate on many issues compared to that of his predecessor. One of these is the role of Rome in the government of the global church, which, compared to his predecessors John Paul II and Benedict XVI, has become less judge and arbiter, more pontifex (bridge builder) within the church and the world.

The issue of church reform has remained on the agenda of Pope Francis: church reform as reform of the way of being church, synodal reform, reform of the universal church and of the particular churches, ecumenical reform, and reform for a more inculturated church.[5] Francis has governed through legislation more than the average Catholic perceives: he has legislated more than Benedict XVI in various areas (for example, reform of marriage tribunals, financial activities of the Holy See, liturgical

---

[3] See Antonio Spadaro, ed., *Il nuovo mondo di Francesco. Come il Vaticano sta cambiando la politica globale* (Padua: Marsilio, 2018).

[4] See Hervè-Marie Legrand, "Le riforme di Francesco," *Il Regno—attualità* 12 (2014): 419–28.

[5] For a wide range of issues representative of the debate on reform in the Catholic Church, see Antonio Spadaro, SJ, and Carlos Maria Galli, eds., *For a Missionary Reform of the Church: The Civiltà Cattolica Seminar*, trans. Demetrio S. Yocum, foreword Massimo Faggioli (Mahwah NJ: Paulist Press, 2017).

norms, resignation of bishops) and in various ways (for example, motu proprio, apostolic constitutions, *rescripta ex audientia*), and he has also created new institutions of government (for example, Council of Cardinals, new Curia dicasteries, commissions with special tasks such as the Pontifical Commission for the Protection of Minors, and—last but not least—the project for a comprehensive overhaul of the Roman Curia).[6] Nevertheless, a gap exists between the developments in the church's teaching and the reluctance of the institutional church—the papacy—to change the Code of Canon Law as part of the different relationship Pope Francis sees between pastoral ministry and canon law.

Collegiality and Synodality versus "the Grasp of Small but Powerful Groups"

The pontificate of Francis began in a church with two opposite forces counterbalancing: the theological and ecclesiological impulse toward decentralization and deinstitutionalization, and the institutional response of the pontificate of Benedict XVI (and of the late part of the pontificate of John Paul II) for a re-institutionalization of the ecclesial dynamics with a strong role played by the Vatican.[7]

On the one side, the demands for a more collegial and synodal church were coming from the defenders of Vatican II as an event and as a source for church reform, while, on the other side, the agenda of a neo-ultramontanist Catholicism was one aspect of the reaction against Vatican II both as a historical memory and as a corpus of documents perceived as a "rupture" in the tradition of the church.

Francis's approach to the issue of the governance of the church has to do with his hermeneutics of the Second Vatican Council. His distance from abstract and idealized hermeneutics of Vatican II shapes his ecclesiology, and in particular his view of collegiality and synodality. Francis is a creative interpreter of

---

[6] See Georg Bier, "Papa Francesco legislatore," *Il Regno—attualità* 22 (2017): 682–85.

[7] See Christoph Theobald, *Accéder à la source*, vol. 1 in *La réception du concile Vatican II* (Paris: Cerf, 2009), 547–654.

Vatican II who sees in the council a dynamic force acting in a globally changing church. His global ecclesiology is clear in his choice of the image of the church as a people over the other image of the church as the body of Christ.[8] Francis's ecclesiology of synodality is rooted in his dynamic use of the *sensus fidei*: "If the *sensus fidei* is a given, we can have access to it, or better, it manifests itself only, in a process of dialogue in an institutional dimension. Here it is necessary to take some distance from a non-dynamic comprehension of the *consensus fidelium* understood only as unanimity within a given expression of the faith."[9] The dynamic comprehension of the *consensus fidelium* in Francis has consequences for his view of the intra-ecclesial dynamics and issues of church governance. Francis's vision of the problem of church governance is cognizant of the theological rifts and ecclesial fault lines of the post–Vatican II era. His discussion of the *affective* and *effective* dimensions of synodal collegiality in his April 1, 2014, letter to Cardinal Lorenzo Baldisseri, secretary general of the Synod of Bishops,[10] is indicative of Francis's honesty in assessing the experiences of the past Synod of Bishops as more affective than effective for most of the members of the world episcopate. Less original was Francis's mention of the need to learn from the synodal model of the Orthodox churches in *Evangelii Gaudium*, in a section on ecumenism, rather than in a discussion of church and decentralization: "In the dialogue with our Orthodox brothers and sisters, we Catholics have the opportunity to learn more about the meaning of episcopal collegiality and their experience of synodality" (no. 246).

---

[8] See Luc Forestier, "Le pape François et la synodalité. *Evangelii gaudium*, nouvelle étape dans la réception de Vatican II," *Nouvelle revue théologique* 13, no. 4 (October 2015): 597–614.

[9] Jean-François Chiron, "Sensus fidei et vision de l'Église chez le Pape François," *Recherches de Science Religieuses* 2016/2 (tome 104): 187–205.

[10] Francis, *Letter to Cardinal Lorenzo Baldisseri, Secretary General of the Synod of Bishops on the occasion of the elevation of Msgr. Fabio Fabene Undersecretary of the Synod to the dignity of bishop*, April 1, 2014, https://w2.vatican.va/content/francesco/en/letters/2014/documents/papa-francesco_20140401_cardinale-baldisseri.html.

But Francis's vision of church governance is to a large extent transversal and "bipartisan" compared to the theological and ecclesial rifts of the post–Vatican II period. For Francis, the rediscovery of a more participative ecclesiological model is not based on a liberal and individualistic idea of a right of the baptized to be consulted and to be part of the decision-making process; rather, it is a missionary ecclesiology. This is clear in the opening paragraphs of *Evangelii Gaudium*:

> I invite all Christians, everywhere, at this very moment, to a renewed personal encounter with Jesus Christ, or at least an openness to letting him encounter them; I ask all of you to do this unfailingly each day. No one should think that this invitation is not meant for him or her, since "no one is excluded from the joy brought by the Lord." (*EG*, no. 3)

It is in this context that the global governance of the church of Francis proceeds toward a less Rome-centered Catholicism:

> I have chosen not to explore these many questions which call for further reflection and study. Nor do I believe that the papal magisterium should be expected to offer a definitive or complete word on every question which affects the church and the world. It is not advisable for the Pope to take the place of local Bishops in the discernment of every issue which arises in their territory. In this sense, I am conscious of the need to promote a sound "decentralization." (*EG*, no. 16)

Reform of church governance, for Francis, is a result of "pastoral conversion" for the missionary effort of the church going forth (*EG*, no. 27). In the same framework of missionary outreach is the self-criticism by the papacy, through Francis, of the failure to realize concretely the wish of Vatican II to make the bishops' conference the subject of collegiality in the church: "Yet this desire has not been fully realized, since a juridical status of episcopal conferences which would see them as subjects of specific attributions, including genuine doctrinal authority, has not yet been sufficiently elaborated. Excessive centralization, rather than proving helpful, complicates the Church's life and her missionary outreach" (*EG*, no. 32).[11] Collegiality and synodality are related to a new appreciation of the charismatic dimension of the church (*EG*, no. 130) and the reliance of the infallibility *in credendo* of the people of God (*EG*, no. 119). Synodality is a missionary synodality: "All the baptized, whatever their position in the Church or their level of instruction in the faith, are agents of evangelization, and it would be insufficient to envisage a plan of evangelization to be carried out by professionals while the rest of the faithful would simply be passive recipients" (*EG*, no. 120).

The issue of collegiality and synodality is no less important in *Laudato Si'*, in which the problem of power is central. The issue of collegiality and synodality is not addressed directly in the encyclical, but it is nonetheless very present, even though indirectly. From a procedural point of view, the choice of developing papal teaching on the basis of teachings of national and continental bishops' conferences is a step from the previous tradition of papal teaching toward a "hermeneutical circle" of reception between papal magisterium and local magisterium. In the argument made in *Laudato Si'* against inequality and exploitation of resources there is a critique of the "technocratic paradigm," which is also a critique of a functionalism in ecclesiology in the form of the reduction of ecclesial dynamics to a corporate-like process that in Catholic culture can take the form of authoritarianism or of facile assimilation of collegiality and synodality to the democratic process in modern liberal democracies.

Laudato Si' shows the interconnectedness of Francis's ecclesiology and social message. It calls for dialogue and transparency in decision-making processes through the involvement of local populations (no. 183). It reminds us that "social problems must be addressed by community networks and not simply by the sum of individual good deeds" (no. 219). *Laudato Si'* is a document on human ecology and on the ecology of power, in the sense of a Christian anthropology of power in technocratic postmodernity. The very choice of the title—*On Our Common Home*—links environment and society, pointing to the mutual interdependence

---

[11] See Carlos Schickendantz, "The Episcopal Conferences: 'This Desire Has Not Been Fully Realized' (EG 32)," in Spadaro and Galli, *For a Missionary Reform of the Church*, 376–99.

and relationships that give priority to fraternity in our attitudes toward both the environment and society.

This ecclesiological response of Francis to the crisis of globalization and to the new Catholic globalization is also a shift in missionary responsibility, from the *institutional* church—bishops and clergy as presiders of local geographical communities—to the *charismatic* and *pneumatological* structure of the church in evangelization.[12] But this shift in responsibility is different from John Paul II's reliance upon charismatic movements and leaders, which was part of his pontificate's effort to maintain the ecclesiastical and clerical status quo.

An even more pronounced emphasis on collegiality and synodality is in the post-synodal exhortation *Amoris Laetitia*. The exhortation not only quotes from ten bishops' conferences (Spain, Korea, Argentina, Mexico, Colombia, Chile, Australia, CELAM, Italy, and Kenya); it also refers to the synods of 2014 and 2015 in a way that reflects the synodal discussions more than any other post-synodal document (more than fifty quotations from the two *relationes*), and it advances its argument for accepting paragraphs of the final *relatio* of 2015 that were approved with a high number of no votes (no. 71 with forty-one no votes, no. 84 with seventy-two no votes, no. 85 with eighty no votes, and no. 86 with sixty-four no votes). From the very beginning of *Amoris Laetitia*, Francis explains his vision of the role of papal magisterium:

> I would make it clear that not all discussions of doctrinal, moral or pastoral issues need to be settled by interventions of the magisterium. Unity of teaching and practice is certainly necessary in the church, but this does not preclude various ways of interpreting some aspects of that teaching or drawing certain consequences from it. This will always be the case as the Spirit guides us toward the entire truth (cf. Jn 16:13), until he leads us fully into the mystery of Christ and enables us to see all things as he does. Each country or region, moreover, can seek solutions better suited to its culture and sensitive to its traditions and local needs. (*AL*, no. 3)

---

[12] See Christoph Theobald, *Fraternità. Il nuovo stile della Chiesa secondo papa Francesco* (Bose: Qiqajon, 2016), 47.

Theological inculturation for Francis is part of the need for a more synodal church. The images of the church used in the synod—"like the beacon of a lighthouse in a port or a torch carried among the people to enlighten those who have lost their way or who are in the midst of a storm," and the "field hospital" (*AL,* no. 291)—are in the context of emergency situations, but these situations are not used to justify authoritarian, hero-like ecclesial leadership. On the contrary, the prophetic voice is relocated to the body of the church. It is not just the specific nature of the exhortation—a document born from a synod is built in order to receive reception from a church in synodality—but it is something that extends to the whole ecclesiology of Francis. This became clear in the address delivered October 17, 2015, during the synod for the fiftieth anniversary of the institution of the Synod of Bishops by Paul VI in 1965. This speech is the most important speech of a pope on synodality in the post–Vatican II church and can be called the *magna carta* of synodality in the postconciliar papal magisterium. Even more important than Francis's articulation of the dimensions of synodality in the various levels in the Catholic Church (in the local and particular churches; in ecclesiastical provinces and ecclesiastical regions, particular councils, and in a special way, conferences of bishops; and at the level of the universal church) is his insertion of the synodal dimension of the church in the context of the global world. In the address Francis said: "The world in which we live, and which we are called to love and serve, even with its contradictions, demands that the church strengthen cooperation in all areas of her mission. It is precisely this path of *synodality* which God expects of the church of the third millennium." Synodality goes to the roots of the tradition: "The Synod of Bishops is the point of convergence of this listening process conducted at every level of the church's life. The Synod process begins by listening to the people of God, which 'shares also in Christ's prophetic office,' according to a principle dear to the church of the first millennium: '*Quod omnes tangit ab omnibus tractari debet.*'"[13]

---

[13] For more on this, see Yves Congar, "Quod omnes tangit ab omnibus tractari et approbari debet," *Revue historique de droit français et étranger* 81 (1958): 210–59.

But at the same time there is in Francis's address a new missionary and ecumenical urgency: "The commitment to build a synodal Church—a mission to which we are all called, each with the role entrusted him by the Lord—has significant ecumenical implications." The last paragraph of the speech is Francis's manifesto for synodality in the global Catholic Church:

> Our gaze also extends to humanity as a whole. A synodal Church is like a standard lifted up among the nations (cf. *Is* 11:12) in a world which—while calling for participation, solidarity and transparency in public administration—often consigns the fate of entire peoples to the grasp of small but powerful groups. As a Church which "journeys together" with men and women, sharing the travails of history, let us cherish the dream that a rediscovery of the inviolable dignity of peoples and of the function of authority as service will also be able to help civil society to be built up in justice and fraternity, and thus bring about a more beautiful and humane world for coming generations.

This acknowledgment of the reversal of positions between the *urbs* and the *orbis* in Catholicism has been clear from the very beginning of Francis's pontificate, with the strong emphasis on the *poor* and on *mercy*, and with synodality as the church's way of responding to "small but powerful groups." Francis is trying to revitalize in the church a synodality that is not merely one that strives to make the church non-monarchical and more collegial; it is also a synodality that ensures that "small but powerful groups" are prohibited from running the church. It is an antidote to those who think that reforming the church requires a well-funded group with abundant travel budgets, connections with the powerful, and effective communication skills. Such a view is complicated because it is not found on only one end of the ideological spectrum. Though it is much more visible on the conservative side, where big money is more easily available than for liberal-progressive causes, both sides of the aisle have become part of this mechanism in different ways. Catholic think tanks and advocacy groups on the liberal end of the spectrum work for issues like gender equality, sexual ethics, lay decision making, and social and economic justice. Those on the conservative end focus on issues like economic freedom, natural family planning, and an anti-LGBT agenda. The conservative groups, especially, do little to take up the cause of those who lack money and power, that is, the poor. Francis's vision of synodality is primarily a call to the church, including theologians who could become tempted to think about their mission as isolated from the church as a people, as he pointed out in his message to participants in an international theological congress held at the Pontifical Catholic University of Argentina (September 1–3, 2015): "[The theologian acknowledges that] the believing People in whom he was born has a theological meaning that he cannot ignore. He knows he is 'plugged' into an ecclesial awareness and immerses himself in those waters." Francis's distance from academic theology is an integral part of his vision of the synodality of the church; clericalism is not just among the clergy. Historically, in the Western world, the privileges of academics and of Catholic clergy have a lot in common.

The global dimension of the Catholic Church constitutes the reason for a real synodality, but is, at the same time, also a challenge. The conditions of the Catholic Church today are significantly different from the times when the reviviscence of collegiality and synodality became visible, that is, at the time of the Second Vatican Council. Globalization of Catholicism means also a church that is more tribal and polarized, globally and locally, in a world that is more interconnected but at the same time also more divided than at the time of Vatican II. The troubles of globalization are also Catholic troubles, with important consequences for the ecclesiology of synodality—the issue of *how* to be synodal.

In this sense Francis's contribution to the development of synodality must be seen in the theological periodization of the debate on collegiality (at Vatican II) and on synodality (in the post–Vatican II church), but also in the context of a larger social and cultural history of Catholicism. Francis's double challenge—a church recovering the promise of collegiality made by Vatican II and the need for synodality expressed by the post–Vatican II church—cannot be assessed in theological and institutional terms only, and it is part of a long-term trajectory.

Reform of the Roman Curia:
Resynchronization More Than Decentralization?

One important aspect—both symbolically and practically—of the issue of the governance of the global church is the central government of the Catholic Church, also known as the Roman Curia. More criticized than actually understood for its entire history, since the early second millennium, the mysteriousness of the Roman Curia is due, in part, to the fact that we know only bits and pieces of its complex and very long history. It is also due to its weak theological foundations, which has forced church leaders, theologians, and ecclesiologists to employ complex arguments in order to explain and justify its existence.

Despite the dark legends surrounding the oldest functioning bureaucracy in the Western world, the Roman Curia is not a monstrosity in the history of Christianity. It is not a deviation from the church's concept of governing and leading the community of the faithful during its history in the West. Significantly, all the popes of the last century—from Pius X to Benedict XVI—confronted the problem of governance and Curia reform. And the way each of them addressed the issue of the Curia was indicative of other key aspects of their pontificates.[14] We now have a similar situation with Pope Francis. Important aspects of his pontificate can be better understood by looking at what he is doing, and *not* doing, with regard to the Roman Curia.

In spring 2019 there was an announcement of the imminent publication of a new apostolic constitution for a reformed Roman Curia to replace the one John Paul II issued in 1988, *Pastor Bonus*. This major reform of the Curia in more than thirty years—a long effort in the making, dating back to the first meetings of the Council of Cardinals between 2013 and 2014—was preceded by an extensive consultation not only with the Curia itself, as in past reforms, but also with the bishops' conferences. The reform of the Roman Curia has accompanied the entire existence of the Council of Cardinals (C9) since its institution by Francis. Italian Bishop Marcello Semeraro, who served as

---

[14] See Massimo Faggioli, "The Roman Curia at and after Vatican II: Legal-Rational or Theological Reform?" *Theological Studies* 76, no. 3 (2015): 550–71.

secretary of C9, published an important article in early 2018 in the Bologna-based Catholic magazine *Il Regno*.[15] Semeraro traces the steps Francis has taken so far to reform some aspects of the Curia (for example, his creation of the Third Section of the Secretariat of State in November 2017). Francis decided not to create the new position of a *moderator Curiae*, a sort of chief administrator of all the offices, because, according to Semeraro, "the analogy between the Roman Curia and the diocesan curia is not appropriate." Moreover, Semeraro outlines several key principles that guide Francis's reform of the Curia. They include the principle of *gradualism* of discernment and experimentations (flexibility); the principle of *tradition* as fidelity to history (no drastic changes); the principle of *innovation* (for example, the new Dicastery for Communication, created between 2015 and 2017); and the principle of *simplification* (merging of dicasteries, but also decentralization). In his article the C9 secretary shows that in Francis's view, the church, the papacy, and the Roman Curia are tightly connected. The Curia exists not only to transmit messages to the rest of the church but also to receive messages from a synodal church. It exists for a Catholic Church not in re-treat but *in* the world, according to Vatican II's *Gaudium et Spes*.

Semeraro offered important insights not just for understanding Pope Francis's work and intention in the reform of the Curia, but also his entire pontificate. For Francis, the Curia's existence is vital for a church that counts on the "Roman genius" on which the Roman Curia has always relied (for better and for worse): that is, the aspiration of Rome to be the synthesis and the point of encounter between the universal-international dimension of the church and the local-particular dimension. The reversal of roles between the former Supreme Congregation of the Holy Office (renamed Congregation for the Doctrine of the Faith after Vatican II) and the Dicastery on Evangelization sums up the priorities in Francis's concept of the Roman Curia in global Catholicism. It amounts also to a reversal of the arrangement of the Roman Curia that was set in the mid-sixteenth century and left untouched until today. This also means a more relevant role for papal diplomacy today than in the previous pontificate; one

---

[15] See Marcello Semeraro, "Riforma della Curia: in atto," *Il Regno— attualità* 2 (2018): 1–7.

of Francis's most interesting decisions has been the meeting of all the papal diplomats in the Vatican every three years (2013, 2016, and 2019).

The repeated delay of the publication of the new apostolic constitution for Francis's reform of the Curia was not a symptom of a fiasco of the C9 or of the pontificate. Rather, it was fully consistent with this pope's approach to the Roman Curia, which has proved to be different from his predecessors' since the first days of his pontificate. "It is attractive to think of the Roman Curia as a small-scale model of the Church, in other words, as a 'body' that strives seriously every day to be more alive, more healthy, more harmonious and more united in itself and with Christ," Francis told Curia officials in his pre-Christmas gathering with them on December 22, 2014. He continues, "In fact, though, the Roman Curia is a complex body, made up of a number of Congregations, Councils, Offices, Tribunals, Commissions, as of numerous elements which do not all have the same task but are coordinated in view of an effective, edifying, disciplined and exemplary functioning, notwithstanding the cultural, linguistic and national differences of its members."

This passage is noteworthy because a key problem of the Curia has always been the questionable nature of its theological legitimacy, in addition to its historic institutional and political functions. But in this address Francis describes the Roman Curia as a "small-scale model of the Church," clearly setting aside the fact that it is fundamentally lacking a basis in ecclesiology and disregarding the differences between, for example, the very diverse sociology of the global church today and the almost totally clerical sociology of the Curia.

Francis has always offered his diagnosis of the problems of the Roman Curia—especially in the dreaded Christmas addresses to the Vatican officials—with language that defines a spiritual experience rather than one that describes functional mismanagement. His non-functionalist approach to the Curia is clearly consistent with his criticism of the "technocratic paradigm" in his 2015 encyclical *Laudato Si'*.

In this respect Francis's handling of the reform of the Roman Curia must be seen in the context of his understanding of the issue of the governance of the global Catholic Church. On the one hand Francis has certainly pushed toward some decentralization of the church, although without investing his pontificate in an institutional decentralization. Most of Francis's efforts have been aimed at stopping and inverting the tendency, evident in the post–Vatican II church of John Paul II and Benedict XVI, to recentralize the church in Rome. Francis made decisions about the authority for liturgical translations (*Magnum Principium*, September 9, 2017) and for the declarations of marriage annulments (*Mitis iudex Dominus Iesus* and *Mitis et misericors Iesus*, both August 15, 2015) that are more restorative than revolutionary from an ecclesiological standpoint. On the other hand, for Francis, decentralization is not just administrative but also magisterial, as demonstrated, for example, in *Amoris Laetitia* (no. 3) and in the geography of his papal trips. From the beginning of his pontificate Francis made clear his disappointment about the centralizing course of Roman Catholicism in the post–Vatican II period. For example, in *Evangelii Gaudium* he writes: "It is not advisable for the Pope to take the place of local Bishops in the discernment of every issue which arises in their territory. In this sense, I am conscious of the need to promote a sound 'decentralization'" (no. 16), and "Excessive centralization, rather than proving helpful, complicates the Church's life and her missionary outreach" (no. 32).

Francis shows a will to decentralize the church, but this will is not disjointed from a fairly classic understanding of the necessity of a central level. Francis does not have in mind a return to the first millennium or to another age as a way of radically reorganizing the structures of the church:

> Francis's "hermeneutic key" is not a plan to reform the church by means of more decentralized structures. . . . We must move into the margins as an experience of Christian living and a starting point for understanding reality. . . . In a globalized world we cannot reproduce the church structure of previous centuries.[16]

---

[16] Andrea Riccardi, *To the Margins: Pope Francis and the Mission of the Church* (Maryknoll, NY: Orbis Books, 2018), 170, original in Italian, *Periferie. Crisi e novità per la Chiesa* (Milan: Jaca Book, 2016).

Rome continues to play a role in Francis's papacy, not least because of the continued visibility of his predecessor, Benedict XVI, as emeritus. Compared to Benedict, Francis has talked more about the Curia and in a different way. In his December 21, 2017, address to the Roman Curia, Francis used the metaphor of Rome as *receiving* and *transmitting* antennae:

> To return to the image of the body, it is fitting to note that these *"institutional senses,"* to which we can in some way compare the Dicasteries of the Roman Curia, must operate in a way befitting their nature and purpose: in the name and with the authority of the Supreme Pontiff, and always for the good and the service of the churches. Within the church, they are called to be like faithful, sensitive antennae: *sending and receiving.*

Overall, Francis's effort has been more about a resynchronization with the peripheries by the antennae of the central government of the Roman Curia than a radical decentralization. It seems that for Francis the new global dimension of the church in the world still needs this kind of antennae as an instrument of communion and communication. The major reform of the Roman Curia proper before the publication of the apostolic constitution had been limited to the merging (which took place between 2014 and 2016) of seven dicasteries into two new dicasteries, one on the laity and one on integral human development. Other reforms decided by Francis have sidelined or bypassed the Curia without ever making an argument for its redundancy. The decision to create the Council of (eight) Cardinals, which was announced on April 13, 2013, and began meeting in October 2013, represents a historical change in the relationship between the pope and the Curia, but without taking away power from Rome and the papacy: in some sense, it has made the central government of the church more centered on the pope and less on the bureaucracy. The inclusion of the cardinal secretary of state (thus making the C8 into the C9) in July 2014 was evidence of the fact that the Council of Cardinals is a governing body emanating from papal power, one whose future after the end of Francis's pontificate is far from clear.

Under Francis, papal Rome has not lost its traditional place: Francis's synods continue to take place in Rome; his new attention to the activity of the Vatican diplomacy is based on the fact that it is a papal diplomacy; his decision to give the pope more power on the resignation of bishops (per papal *Rescritto* of November 5, 2014) is an indication that the church's government is still centered in Rome; and the location in the Vatican of the new judicial body within the Congregation for the Doctrine of the Faith to handle appeals by priests who have been disciplined for sexually abusing children (decision announced November 11, 2014) is an indication that on critical issues Rome is still seen as the natural place for the decision-making process involving the whole church. This is part not only of keeping with the tradition, but also of Francis's pedagogy of reform: the pontificate of Francis has revealed the paradox that the decentralization of the global governance of the Catholic Church needs heavy Vatican inputs.

During Francis's pontificate Rome has been the central point of a spiritual reform of the church that requires a spiritual reform of the Curia, but also a different relationship with the magisterial dimension of the Vatican:

> There is a transition from a cumulative approach, concerned with always giving due consideration to the dogmatic content of the Christian faith, to a procedural and relational approach centered on the offering of the Gospel of Jesus Christ. . . . Here there are profound consequences on the plan of the form of the church and its relationship with the world.[17]

Compared to his immediate predecessor, Francis is inverting the trend of the relationship between the Roman Curia and the church, from a dogmatic understanding of the government of the church to a kerygmatic one.

---

[17] Gianfranco Brunelli, "Convertire le strutture," *Il Regno—attualità* 22 (2016): 642.

Catholic Globalization and Its Discontents

An analysis of Francis's handling of church governance requires nuancing, given Francis's ecclesiology of reform, which is aimed more at a conversion of the mentality of bureaucrats than at institutional reform of the bureaucratic structures. Francis is animated by the idea of church reform articulated by Yves Congar before Vatican II, especially in *True and False Reform*.[18] Congar emphasized the primacy of charity and of pastorality; the preservation of communion; patience with and respect for delays; and renewal through return to the principle of tradition. This makes the ecclesial politics of Francis's pontificate more complicated, because Congar's idea of church reform can be frustrating for those who have lost the patience Congar was invoking fifty years ago. Many Catholic experts and theologians expect a visible institutional reform of the Curia, but this expectation reflects a technocratic mentality that Francis does not share.

During the first six years of his pontificate, Francis did not emphasize the need for a bureaucratic overhaul of the central government of the Catholic Church, and there is a difference between him and the predecessors that are theologically closer to him: John XXIII called the council on January 25, 1959, less than three months after his election, in an act that was in itself one way of addressing the issue of the Roman Curia and its role in the global church; Paul VI reformed the Curia four years after his election, with the apostolic constitution *Regimini Ecclesiae Universae* of August 15, 1967. Francis's approach to the issue of the Roman Curia has been shaped by looking at it not from the center—as was typical of his predecessors—but from the peripheries and from the global church. There is thus a difference in the perceived emergencies and in the solutions.

The issue of the reform of the Roman Curia and of church governance was quite high on the list of expectations at the beginning of Francis's pontificate, in a global church where the mentality of the single-issue reform agenda has become more influential than in the past. One of the major changes we have

---

[18] Yves Congar, *True and False Reform in the Church*, trans. Paul Philibert, OP (Collegeville, MN: Liturgical Press, 2010), original in French (Paris: Cerf, 1950).

seen in the last several years—not just in politics, but also in the church—is the growing influence of advocacy groups, lobbies, and think tanks. Among the liberal-progressive Catholics "disappointed" by Pope Francis, there are those who reproach him for not having kept the promises of modernization of the church's bureaucratic apparatus.[19] In a certain sense the way Francis has approached the issue of institutional reform is representative of his whole pontificate: too revolutionary for the standard bearer of the status quo, and too traditional for so-called revolutionaries and their agenda for Francis's papacy. This is not a centrist position that is ideologically confusing for the entrenched fronts of ideological Catholicism. In part, it is the impossibility of framing Francis in the liberal-versus-conservative scheme, especially for the institutional issues in Catholicism. But it is also part of the evolution of the papal ministry. Governing the church from Rome can be seen as a formidable task for an evangelizer against centuries of stratified institutional baggage, but it also can be seen as a cautionary tale against the worldly fetish of the pope superstar, a solitary hero, and a miracle worker. The messianic expectations for the bishop of Rome are tested by the Roman Curia: the resilience of the Vatican bureaucracy can be interpreted simplistically as the fight for the preservation of the power of Rome. But this reluctance of the central government in the Vatican to be reformed or to reform itself can also serve the healthy purpose of bringing expectations about leadership in the Catholic Church back to reality.

The real question for the future of the global Catholic Church is not the reform or reformability of the Roman Curia, but the ability of the rest of the church to support the development of a global church that cannot and will not rely on Rome as it did in the past, in a more Europe-centered Catholic Church. In other words, the real question is about the "Francis effect" on the local churches, and especially on the national and continental bishops' conferences, and from them on the seminaries for the formation of priests and the schools of theology and ministry. The vision of Francis for a globalization of the College of Cardinals has

---

[19] See, for example, Marco Marzano, *La Chiesa immobile. Francesco e la rivoluzione mancata* (Rome-Bari: Laterza, 2018).

been a success; Bergoglio's rupture with the historical criterion of traditional cardinal sees (thus making space for new cardinals from the global south and younger churches all over the world, especially from Africa and Asia) has made possible a departure from the previous models of representation of the church through the composition of the electoral college of the bishop of Rome.[20] As of 2019, the 120 cardinals eligible to enter a conclave came from sixty-five countries, compared to forty-eight nations represented at the conclave that elected John Paul II and fifty-two at the conclave that elected Benedict XVI. The same can be said about the appointments of bishops, which under Francis have been chosen from priests with a visibly pastoral profile and not from clerics from administrative or academic backgrounds.

But the issue of the reform of the life of the local churches remains an open question. The pontificate of Francis and the reactions to its evangelical appeal, to the gospel *sine glossa*—without too much cultural mediation—has shown that the real challenge is more than the reform of the institution. It is, in the words of the Italian theologian Giuseppe Ruggieri, "the re-appropriation of the church as an experience of brotherhood and sisterhood."[21] The discontents of Catholic globalization are more about a more fractured sense of the church than about the inability to reform the structures. The keys to this synodal sense of the church— *liturgy*, *poverty*, and *mercy*—have been the most difficult for Francis to transmit to the neoconservative and neo-traditionalist Catholicism that is now, two generations after Vatican II, an integral part of the Catholic landscape in the West in dealing with the globalization of the church. The neo-traditionalist insurgency will have an impact on the agenda of the church and also on one aspect—the reform of the Roman Curia—on which Catholic neo-traditionalists tend to be more agnostic than on other issues (liturgical, canonical, moral-theological).

Those who try to understand the issue of reform of the governance of the global church have found in Francis's pontificate an important opportunity for understanding the development

---

[20] See especially the consistories for the creation of new cardinals of February 22, 2014, February 14, 2015, and November 19, 2016.

[21] Giuseppe Ruggieri, *Chiesa sinodale* (Rome-Bari: Laterza, 2017), 170.

of the problem. If Benedict XVI's decision to resign was also due to a failure in his ability to control the central government of the church, Francis's pontificate has shown that the crisis went deeper than one particular pope. Francis is the pope of a newly globalized church in the sense that the globalization of the church means the transition from the functionalist dream of some institutional reforms of Vatican II[22]—the council worked with the idea of the existence of an institutional fix to the problems of Catholicism (for example, the decision to set a retirement age for bishops)—to the reality of governing an institution that could become much less reliant on laws and regulations and much more on its charismatic element.

Francis's pontificate also has been about the relationship between the expectations for a pope to be a reformer of the institution and the fact that the Roman papacy has become a charismatic role. Whatever the institutionalization of the papacy tried to control in the charismatization of the papal role since the First Vatican Council of 1869–70 (by means of the declarations on papal primacy and papal infallibility), the papacy now embodies a power that is more charismatic than institutional.

Paradoxically, one of the discontents of this Catholic globalization comes from the awareness of the growing evidence of the limits of papal power in the church of today. The internationalization of the Roman Curia dreamed of by Vatican II and launched by Paul VI has been made real in Pope Francis by symbolically restructuring the relationship between the pope and the global church by creating more distance between the pope and the Curia, its Roman and Italian historical-political environment. The papacy of Francis has been more focused on the chaotic and multicultural and multi-religious city of Rome than on the holy city, papal Rome; more focused on Italian Catholics and Christians than on the Italian bishops' conference or Italian politics.

This is a consequence of what one could call, paraphrasing Claude Lévi-Strauss's famous memoir *Tristes Tropiques,* the sad part of the Catholic globalization. It is a globalization more affected by ethno-nationalism and tribalism not only in the social

---

[22] See Giovanni Sale, SJ, "La riforma della Curia Romana. Dal Concilio Vaticano II ai nostri giorni," *La Civiltà Cattolica,* 3998 (January 14–28, 2017): 105–19.

and political sphere, but also in the church. One example is the case of Peter Okpaleke, who was appointed bishop of the southern Nigerian diocese of Ahiara by Benedict XVI in 2012, but who was never able to take possession of the diocese because of the widespread nature of local protests. This is an example of the new and visible difficulty of papal power in winning over fragmented ecclesial identities. Bishop Okpaleke had to resign in February 2018, despite Francis's strong exhortation to his local church in his "Address to a Delegation from the Diocese of Ahiara, Nigeria" of June 8, 2017, to accept him as a bishop. The pope backed down in a dispute with Nigerian priests who had complained that Okpaleke was not from Mbaise, the region surrounding their diocese, and Francis accepted the bishop's resignation.

The discontents of Catholic globalization are not surfacing only from those parts of the Catholic globe that have acquired new visibility in the age of the interconnected church. It is now part of the life of Catholicism in larger areas of the world. The phenomenon of the new Catholic traditionalism must be understood also as a reaction against multicultural globalization and also against Catholic globalization. This fragmentation has been amplified by the virtualization of Catholicism—the creation of religious identities in cyberspace—and by the legacy of the institutional sclerosis of the church under the guidance of John Paul II and Benedict XVI, marked by the inability not only to live synodally but also to believe in the very idea of a church that can debate synodally. Synodal government of the church proves particularly difficult when the diplomatic activities of the Holy See are concerned.

In the same respect, the current disruption of globalization reflects the polar tensions of *globalization* and *localization* in Jorge Mario Bergoglio. For example, the September 2018 agreement between the Holy See and the People's Republic of China has led to a particular form of discontent among some Chinese Catholic leaders—that is, discontent with globalization and with the Vatican handling of it through an agreement with the government of mainland China. This is important because the Chinese Catholic context is changing the way we look at the relationship between ecclesiology of the *local* and *universal* church. In light of the aggressive claims of the Chinese government on the control of religion, Francis's approach to the Catholic situation in China shows how the present stage of globalization compels the church to rethink an often unilateral endorsement of the ecclesiology of the local church as the most important trajectory of the post–Vatican II church.

In an age of rising nationalism, as well as polarization within the Catholic Church itself, the global governance of the church problem depends much more on the peripheries than on the center. The true transition to a synodal church depends on how much the church around the world is willing to accept and support this new kind of church governance. Catholicism today still flirts with the dangerous tendency to rely on one man only: the pope. Francis's pontificate certainly offers an interesting example of leadership in an age of fascination with the "strongman."

Governance of the Global Church and the Sexual-Abuse Crisis

One of the areas where Francis has resisted the temptation and the pressure to act as a "strongman" and to call for a "law-and-order" papacy is in his handling of the sexual-abuse crisis in the Catholic Church. Indeed, the handling of this global scandal has been one of the areas where Francis's spiritual governance of the Catholic Church through discernment has been met with impatience.

For what concerns a study on the globalization of Catholicism, it is relevant to note that it is during Pope Francis's papacy that the crisis of the abuses committed by Catholic clergy has become a global Catholic crisis *also* in the perception of the Vatican. The unprecedented meeting of all presidents of the bishops' conferences in the Vatican (February 21–24, 2019) was a key moment for understanding the paradoxical tension between the need to decentralize the Catholic Church and at the same time to call the church to a decentralizing reform from the center.

The phenomenon of the crisis and the response to the crisis have shown the particularities of the Catholic Church as a global church, but also as an international organization in which the religious-spiritual and political-diplomatic realms are never completely separated. The sex-abuse crisis in the Catholic Church has tested the logic of the church's structure much more than any organization investigated for the same pattern of criminal behavior, and much more than other churches and religious groups. But it has also tested the ecclesiological model of governance of the post–Vatican II church.

The sex-abuse crisis in the Catholic Church is multilayered: a problem of corruption (crimes and cover-ups); a problem of credibility of official teaching on sexual morality; and a problem of diversity in the Catholic Church as it deals with issues of gender and sexuality.[23] But the sex-abuse crisis has also revealed the unsustainability of an ecclesiological model that in the second post–Vatican II period (between John Paul II and Benedict XVI) frustrated the theological role at the local and national level. In this sense Francis's action on the sex-abuse crisis has been a mix of necessary central impulses—from the creation of the Pontifical Commission for the Abuse of Minors in 2014 to the decision to call the meeting of all presidents of bishops' conferences and major superiors of religious orders in February 2019—and of a new opening of spaces for collegiality and synodality. This is a mix that reflects not only the ecclesiology of Pope Francis, but also the need for a reexamination of the universal-central and local levels of Roman Catholicism.

There is no question that Pope Francis's ecclesiological rebalancing has challenged the centralization of the previous pontificates, with a generation of bishops who were previously appointed and promoted on the basis of different ecclesiological priorities. But it is an open question—for the handling of the sex-abuse crisis but more for the governance of the Catholic Church in general—what kind of balance this will be. The sex-abuse crisis has had, and will likely continue to have, a major impact on a wide range of ecclesiological issues, including the relationships between church and state, between clergy and laity, and between local churches and Rome. In terms of the institutional church's handling of the sex-abuse crisis, strategies for fighting clerical sexual abuse began with Benedict XVI. But the discourse on collegiality and synodality as ecclesiological conversions necessary

---

[23] See Massimo Faggioli, "The Catholic Church's Biggest Crisis since the Reformation," *Foreign Affairs* (October 11, 2018).

to fight against clericalism as a root cause of the sexual abuse in the church began with Pope Francis.

The years 2018 and 2019 inaugurated a new phase in the history of the Catholic sex-abuse crisis, as seen in the defrocking of former cardinal Theodore McCarrick and the convictions of Cardinal George Pell by an Australian tribunal for crimes of sexual abuse against minors and of Cardinal Philippe Barbarin by a French tribunal for failing to report an abusive priest, which together mark a new chapter in the relations between church and state. Spring 2019 made clear the unprecedented complexity of the crisis and the role of the papacy in it. From the entourage of Benedict XVI, on April 10, 2019, emerged an essay interpreting the genesis of the sexual-abuse crisis—a counter narrative that directly fed opposition to Pope Francis. The sex-abuse crisis has become a test for the Catholic Church in globalization also because it strikes at the heart of a deep contradiction within the Catholic theology of these last sixty years: on the one side, the realization that the Catholic Church has never been as centralized as it is; and on the other side, the consciousness that in church history major processes of reform always need a certain amount of centralization. Or, in the words of Yves Congar: "Historically, centralization has been a necessity and a good thing."[24] But the cohabitation between Francis and his predecessor in the Vatican II has complicated the question of what centralization in the Catholic Church truly is.

---

[24] Congar, *True and False Reform in the Church*, 262.

6

The Papacy, Geopolitics, and the Crisis of Globalization

The loss of temporal power due to the extinction of the Papal States and the secularization of the Western world, the historical cradle of Christianity, have given birth to an internationally and diplomatically more active papacy. It is important to note that the Second Vatican Council has not completely superseded Vatican I: the elevation of the papacy to the global stage and the modernity (even though an anti-liberal modernity) of the council called by Pius IX continue to shape to a large extent the office of the bishop of Rome in the global world.[1]

During the last century the diplomatic activity of the Holy See and of the papacy has expanded significantly, augmenting the peculiar "political" specificity of the Roman Catholic Church compared to all the other churches and religions. At the end of Pius X's pontificate in 1914, the Holy See had diplomatic relations with 14 states.[2] In 1978, the number of states with which the Holy See had full diplomatic relations numbered 84; in 2005, there were 174; and in 2018, 183. There are 89 embassy chanceleries based in Rome, including those of the European Union and the Sovereign Military Order of Malta. The offices of the League

---

[1] See Emile Perreau-Saussine, *Catholicism and Democracy: An Essay in the History of Political Thought* (Princeton, NJ: Princeton University Press, 2012), original in French (Paris: Cerf, 2011).

[2] See John Pollard, *The Papacy in the Age of Totalitarianism, 1914–1958* (Oxford: Oxford University Press, 2014), 23–27.

of Arab States, the International Organization for Migration, and the United Nations High Commission for Refugees are also based in Rome.[3] The city of Rome has an international presence that is unparalleled in other cities that have played an important role in the two-thousand-year-long history of Christianity. This expansion of the diplomatic activity of the Holy See and of papal diplomacy was a trend that has accompanied all the popes of the twentieth century, thanks also to the new wave of Catholic internationalism after World War I.[4] Despite all the differences between the papacies of the early twentieth century and those of the late twentieth century, it is undeniable that they all represented and embodied a Catholic Church still expressive of a Europe-centered Christianity dealing with the end of the tight relationship between the church and empires: the "Christian" empires in Europe until World War I (German, Austrian, and Russian); the "Christian" colonial empires until World War II and its aftermath (France, Belgium, Great Britain, and Italy); and the Communist empire versus the anti-Communist Western front during the Cold War until 1989–91.[5] Benedict XVI's papacy was in some sense one of transition. He was elected in 2005, the first conclave of the post–9/11 era, and interpreted his role as claiming a special relationship among Christianity, Europe, and the Western hemisphere.[6]

---

[3] Holy See Press Office, "Note on the Diplomatic Relations of the Holy See," January 8, 2018.

[4] See *Christdemokratie in Europa im 20. Jahrhundert—Christian Democracy in 20th-Century Europe—La Démocratie Chrétienne en Europe au XXe siècle*, ed. Michael Gehler, Wolfram Kaiser, and Helmut Wohnout (Vienna: Böhlau, 2001).

[5] See Leo Kenis et al., *The Transformation of the Christian Churches in Western Europe 1945–2000* (Leuven: Leuven University Press, 2010); *World Christianities c. 1914–c. 2000*, vol. 9 of *The Cambridge History of Christianity*, ed. Hugh McLeod (Cambridge: Cambridge University Press, 2006).

[6] See, for example, Joseph Ratzinger, "Europe: Heritage with Obligations for Christians," in *Church, Ecumenism, and Politics: New Essays in Ecclesiology* (New York: Crossroad, 1988), 221–36; Joseph Ratzinger with Marcello Pera, *Without Roots: The West, Relativism, Christianity, Islam* (New York: Basic Books, 2006).

With the election of Pope Francis, the geopolitical and diplomatic vision of the Catholic Church has been given a new voice and a new face in a historical and geopolitical situation different from the one faced by his immediate predecessors. Thanks to Francis, the cosmopolitan and international dimension of Catholicism has emerged as particularly distinctive, in comparison to the *Zeitgeist* of walls and borders, typical of the disruption of globalization.[7] Francis is the first pope in modern church history born in a multicultural capital, located in the southern hemisphere, and one of the most important destinations on the map of global migrations in the first half of the twentieth century. Francis has introduced the world to a particularly Catholic imagination of space, and he has introduced Western Catholics to a new global imagination of the space of the church.[8]

As we have seen in the previous chapters, Pope Francis is a product of globalization seen through the eyes of a capital city of the southern hemisphere, full of contradictions and paradoxes. Not only his spirituality, but also his views of history and of the role of Christians, of the church, and of the Holy See are inseparable from this background. But there is also a theology and an ecclesiology of Pope Francis that shape his view of the international activity of the Catholic Church, of the Holy See, and of papal diplomacy.

Francis's Post-Constantinian Church and International Affairs

Francis's theology proceeds from the view that the church is fundamentally a people gathered by Jesus Christ, in which the institutional dimension has an important but limited role; the different roles within the people must be seen in light of a radical

---

[7] See Massimo Faggioli, "La crisi della globalizzazione cattolica. Chiesa e politica dal Vaticano II a Francesco," *Il Mulino* 67, no. 5 (2018): 846–54.

[8] See Andrea Riccardi, *La sorpresa di papa Francesco. Crisi e futuro della Chiesa* (Milan: Mondadori, 2013), 130.

equality that does not necessarily require institutional changes but absolutely requires spiritual conversion.

In Francis's ecclesiology, imbalance and abuse of power in the church cannot be solved with a response of power. One of the aspects of conversion is connected to power dynamics inside the church, but also with political power outside of the church. Francis does not see the need for political power to protect the church; in church history, protection has always implied subjugation.[9] This is the foundation of Francis's rejection of the temptations of Constantinianism.[10] Francis rejects the idea of Catholicism as an empire—political, cultural, or civilizational.[11] This is visible from the fact that Francis has little theological use for the concept of borders, of frontiers, not only between churches and religions, but also between nations and peoples. In contrast, his preferred metaphors have to do with spaces in between—dialogue, encounter, peripheries, and bridges, rather than walls.[12]

This does not mean that Francis has a naive perception of the international situation. In his pontificate, he has been willing to be present on the international scene and to take political risks more than his immediate predecessor, Benedict XVI. A theologically and magisterially activist papacy, Benedict XVI's, has been followed by a less activist theologically but internationally more activist papacy, Francis's, which has been affected by such world events as: the failure of the Arab Spring and the chaos in the Middle East (especially Syria); the turn of Latin America to populist right-wing leaders and the failure of progressive politics; the crisis of the European Union and the protracted political psychosis of Brexit (since spring 2016); the rise of nationalism

---

[9] See Walter Ullmann, *The Growth of Papal Government in the Middle Ages: A Study in the Ideological Relation of Clerical to Lay Power* (London: Methuen, 1955), 1–43.

[10] See José Luis Narvaja, "La crisi di ogni politica cristiana. Erich Przywara e l'"idea di Europa,'" *La Civiltà Cattolica*, 3977 (March 12, 2016), 437–48.

[11] Antonio Spadaro, "Sfida all'apocalisse," in *Il nuovo mondo di Francesco. Come il Vaticano sta cambiando la politica globale*, ed. Antonio Spadaro (Padua: Marsilio, 2017), 42–43.

[12] About Francis's vocabulary, see *A Pope Francis Lexicon*, ed. Joshua McElwee and Cindy Wooden (Collegeville, MN: Liturgical Press, 2018).

and ethnicism in the Western world; and the conquest of global powers competing with Europe and North America (such as Brazil, Russia, India, and China) by "strongmen." Francis's world is a world that is unexpected if we compare it to the expectations following the victory of John Paul II over communism or the immediate post–9/11 world of Benedict XVI. During the pontificate of Benedict XVI we could only see the beginning of the reversal of the high tide of liberal democracies, the crisis of the open and multicultural world order, and the rise of identity politics within the Western hemisphere and in countries important for the geopolitics of Christianity and Catholicism. During Francis's pontificate the crisis has become visible in its global and systemic features.

Francis does not engage in a systematic analysis of the crises of democracies, but he is keenly aware of the violent conflict marking the international situation: "The fundamental datum that Francis' papacy assumes in looking at international politics is conflict. . . . The pontificate of Francis is dramatic because he knows he lives in a conflict that cannot be stopped as a constitutive and inevitable fact of human history."[13] Francis's response to the global crisis is not a retreat or a defense, however. As he said to the community of writers of *Civiltà Cattolica* on February 9, 2017, "Only a truly open thought can face the crisis and the understanding of where the world is going, of how to tackle the most complex and urgent crises, the geopolitical issues, the challenges of the economy and the serious humanitarian crisis linked to the tragedies of migration, which is the true global political knot of our day."

This open thinking by Francis means a de-sacralization of power—including political power—in the sense of the acceptance of the basic nakedness of the mechanisms of power struggles. It's a rejection of any political Manicheism in favor of an ecumenism that is intra-ecclesial but also interreligious and political, and it requires the pope to dialogue with everybody and anybody: Donald Trump and Vladimir Putin, Nicolás Maduro and the president of Iran Rouhani, Raul Castro and the generals of the junta in Myanmar, the Grand Imam Ahmed el-Tayeb of Al-Azhar in Cairo and Abu Dhabi's crown prince, Sheikh Mohammed bin

---

[13] Spadaro, "Sfida all'apocalisse," 13.

Zayed al-Nahyan. It also means avoiding forcing the church into strategic alliances with political actors or nations, including those who think of themselves as natural allies of Christianity and of the church.[14] Francis rejects both the theory of the "clash of civilizations"[15] and the idea of the church as an ideological refuge from the clash, from "the revenge of God" and the comeback of religions in the crisis of secularism,[16] but also from secular modernity in the Western hemisphere.

In this sense we must use caution when using the term *soft-power superpower* to talk about the international activity of the Holy See and papal diplomacy, because it can entail the projection on the Catholic Church of a spirit and of intentions that are not its own.[17] The church's power is not the same soft power of other international organizations' agency; yet the Catholic Church can still rely on a network of institutions and organizations that can be seen as more successful in delivering help than in driving cultural change.

Vatican Europeism in the Crisis of the European Union

Pope Francis's pontificate is very expressive of Jorge Mario Bergoglio's worldview and his response to the disruption of globalization, as he continually reemphasizes the diplomatic tradition of the Holy See. It is clear that there is a shifting geopolitics of the papacy toward a new sense of global Catholicism, one that is less constrained by the parameters of the historical roots of Christianity and more oriented toward the new processes taking place in the church worldwide.

---

[14] Ibid., 17–18.

[15] See Samuel Huntington, *The Clash of Civilizations and the Remaking of World Order* (New York: Simon and Schuster, 1996).

[16] See Gilles Kepel, *The Revenge of God: The Resurgence of Islam, Christianity, and Judaism in the Modern World* (University Park: Pennsylvania State University Press, 1994).

[17] For the concept of soft power, see Joseph S. Nye, Jr., *Soft Power: The Means to Success in World Politics* (New York: Public Affairs, 2004).

What is still unclear is the sustainability of the magnitude of the shift in the church after Francis. This shift is not merely the swinging of the theological pendulum produced by a conclave in response to the previous conclave and the pontiff it elected. It is about the kind of relationship that will develop, in the long run, between the turn of Roman Catholicism toward the global south and its Roman center—with all the consequences on the international dimension of a Holy See that is still based institutionally and symbolically in Rome. Francis has re-signified and reinterpreted the power in and of papal Rome, but he has not renounced or diminished the role of Rome. It is only from Rome that the redrawing of the map could proceed, but a Rome understood from the extreme ends of the world and for a wider Catholic world.[18]

The entire pontificate of Francis has been a reinterpretation of the world that includes Rome and of course Italy and Europe. Some key moments during the pontificate have been particularly expressive of Francis's vision of Europe, such as those in spring 2016: the trip to the Greek island of Lesbos to visit a refugee camp (with His Holiness Bartholomew, ecumenical patriarch of Constantinople, and His Beatitude Ieronymos, archbishop of Athens and all Greece) in April; the acceptance of the Charlemagne Prize (the prestigious *Karlspreis*, the oldest and best-known prize awarded for work done in the service of European unification) with an audience in the Vatican with the leaders of the European Union on May 6; and the interview with the French Catholic magazine *La Croix*, also in May 2016.

Upon receiving the Charlemagne Prize, Francis articulated in his address of May 6, 2016, a vision of Europe that is not nostalgic for the Catholic-run Christian Democratic parties ruling the European Union in the early post–World War II period, but rather called Europe to a "new humanism." He talked about a Europe "capable of giving birth to a new humanism based on three capacities: the capacity to integrate, the capacity for dialogue and the capacity to generate." He made clear references to

---

[18] See Antonio Spadaro, "Lo sguardo di Magellano. L'Europa, Papa Francesco, e il Premio Carlo Magno," *Civiltà Cattolica*, 3983 (June 11, 2016): 469–79.

the need for a different economic model: "a new, more inclusive and equitable economic model, aimed not at serving the few, but at benefiting ordinary people and society as a whole. This calls for moving from a liquid economy to a social economy."

On April 16, 2016, in his meeting with the people of Lesbos and the Catholic community, Francis called Europe to its responsibility: "Europe is the homeland of human rights, and whoever sets foot on European soil ought to sense this, and thus become more aware of the duty to respect and defend those rights." At the end of that day, Francis rescued twelve Muslim refugees from that detention camp and took them to Rome on the papal flight, an extraordinary privilege available to the pope as the sovereign of the Vatican City State.

In an interview with *La Croix*, on May 17, 2016, Francis explained with great clarity his view of the relationship between Europe and Christianity:

> We need to speak of roots in the plural because there are so many. In this sense, when I hear talk of the Christian roots of Europe, I sometimes dread the tone, which can seem triumphalist or even vengeful. It then takes on colonialist overtones. John Paul II, however, spoke about it in a tranquil manner. Yes, Europe has Christian roots and it is Christianity's responsibility to water those roots. But this must be done in a spirit of service as in the washing of the feet. Christianity's duty to Europe is one of service. As Erich Przywara, the great master of Romano Guardini and Hans Urs von Balthasar, teaches us, Christianity's contribution to a culture is that of Christ in the washing of the feet. In other words, service and the gift of life. It must not become a colonial enterprise.

Francis's position on the Christian character of Europe and on European Christianity must be seen in the context of the attempted ideological reclamation of the Christian roots of the continent in these last few years, especially in Central and Eastern Europe, once the center of Catholic Europe, in the Habsburg Empire earlier and in anti-Russian and anti-Communist Christian Europe later (Austria, Poland, and Hungary). European politicians have now repurposed the Christian roots of Europe in anti-immigrant and anti-Muslim fashion. In his "Address to the Heads of State and Government of the European Union," on March 24, 2017 (the sixtieth anniversary of the Rome Treaties), Francis reminded these leaders:

> At the origin of the idea of Europe, we find "the nature and the responsibility of the human person, with his ferment of evangelical fraternity . . . with his desire for truth and justice, honed by a thousand-year-old experience." Rome, with its vocation to universality, symbolizes that experience and was thus chosen as the place for the signing of the Treaties.

Francis then connected his bridge-building geopolitics with the intent of the European Union:

> In a world that was all too familiar with the tragedy of walls and divisions, it was clearly important to work for a united and open Europe, and for the removal of the unnatural barrier that divided the continent from the Baltic Sea to the Adriatic. What efforts were made to tear down that wall! Yet today the memory of those efforts has been lost.

Pope Francis and the United States: Ecclesial and Geopolitical Issues

Francis has talked about the political and spiritual crises of Europe as part of the global landscape of his pontificate, without viewing Europe as the critically necessary heartland for the future of Catholicism or Christianity. Francis's geopolitics must be seen in the context of the geography of the opposition to the pontificate, not only in Europe but also across the North Atlantic.[19] Paradoxically, the first pope from the Americas has contributed to making the Atlantic wider between Europe and

---

[19] See Marco Politi, *Pope Francis among the Wolves: The Inside Story of a Revolution*, trans. William McCuaig (New York: Columbia University Press, 2015), original in Italian (Rome-Bari: Laterza, 2014).

the new continent, especially North America.[20] This has been an element of change of historic proportion, considering the special bonds between the historical and cultural cradle of Roman Catholicism and its continental offspring generated by migrations of non-Catholic religious dissenters in the seventeenth century and Catholic economic migrants from European and non-European countries later in the nineteenth and twentieth centuries. Francis's papacy has seen a growing division among the Catholic churches in the Americas—North, Central, and South. But Francis has cast a light on the growing distance between the Vatican and North American Catholicism in a particular way. From the point of view of the cultural and institutional history of Catholicism, the relationship between the Roman Catholic Church in the United States and Europe, Italy, and the Vatican has always been a revelation of the profound movements within this immigrant religion (especially from Europe, Latin America, and Asia) and its shifting geopolitics.[21]

Both Pope Francis and Donald Trump have helped to make the Atlantic wider. What unites Francis and Trump is a change in the vision of Europe. Both for Trump's White House and for the Holy See of Francis, Europe no longer has the same role it had for its predecessors, both as a continent and as a European Union. From the Vatican point of view, the new global dimension of the pontificate and of the church of Pope Francis has increased the distance between the idea of Catholicism and Europe.

On the other hand, if the presidency of Donald Trump has increased the distance between the United States and Europe (for example, on NATO and international alliances, on the social and economic model), he has also signaled a greater distance between

---

[20] Here my thesis differs significantly from that of Manlio Graziano, *In Rome We Trust: The Rise of Catholics in American Political Life* (Stanford, CA: Stanford University Press, 2017), original in Italian, *In Rome We Trust. L'ascesa dei cattolici nella vita politica degli Stati Uniti* (Bologna: Il Mulino, 2016).

[21] See Peter R. D'Agostino, *Rome in America: Transnational Catholic Ideology from the Risorgimento to Fascism* (Chapel Hill: University of North Carolina Press, 2004); Luca Castagna, *A Bridge across the Ocean: The United States and the Holy See between the Two World Wars* (Washington, DC: Catholic University of America Press, 2014), original in Italian (Bologna: Il Mulino, 2011).

the United States and the Vatican on the question of globalization. Catholicism still proposes itself as a form of universalism and internationalism that no longer finds an important interlocutor in the American presidency. The support offered to the Trump presidency by some US Catholic sectors is one of the ways US Catholicism has distanced itself from the political cultures of the Second Vatican Council and from the universalism and internationalism of Catholic social doctrine. It is also clearly a way to distance US Catholicism from Pope Francis's pontificate. Francis's social and moral teachings have raised eyebrows and led to open criticism in small but influential circles of Catholicism in the United States, reinforcing the self-perception of part of the American Catholic church as part of a new so-called moral majority within global Catholicism. In a different way from the era of the pontificates of John Paul II and Benedict XVI, conservative Catholicism in the United States is now one of the factors of this greater distance between the United States and the Vatican, and no longer or not necessarily a factor of containment of the global forces that push the Vatican and the United States in different directions.

Between the vision of Pope Francis and that of President Trump's America there are numerous elements of tension and opposition that represent a novelty in the history of relations between the Holy See and the White House, at least from the Second World War onward. This also entails a different vision of the role of the United States in world history between Francis and his predecessors; Francis sees no especially providential role for the United States in world history and in global Christianity. If Francis's vision has a providential role for America, it is for Latin America and the irruption of the poor in world history, not for North America.[22]

---

[22] See Massimo Borghesi, *The Mind of Pope Francis: Jorge Mario Bergoglio's Intellectual Journey*, trans. Barry Hudock (Collegeville, MN: Liturgical Press, 2018), original in Italian, *Jorge Mario Bergoglio. Una biografia intellettuale* (Milan: Jaca Book, 2017), 53–61; Massimo Faggioli, "Un problema americano per il papa dalla fine del mondo?," in *Limes. Rivista italiana di geopolitica* 3 (2014): 169–76; and idem, "Francesco e Trump, convergenze parallele," in *Limes. Rivista italiana di geopolitica* 7 (2017): 191–97.

It is within this framework that the most important intervention of Francis's diplomacy must be seen, that is, in the relations between the United States and Cuba in December 2014, a few months before Francis's visit to the United States in September 2015 (during President Obama's administration).[23] Francis sees the world map in motion and with no settled center of gravity, certainly not a center of gravity in the northern hemisphere or in North America. This creates a counter narrative to the narrative and imagery of an Anglo-American Catholicism as the best or only part of the global church able to stem the tide of secularism and the anthropological challenge. In fact, Francis's sociopolitical message can be seen as exactly the opposite of Christian ethnonationalisms typical of the crisis of globalization, including the attempts to justify theologically the ideology of America First.

This is why the most significant transatlantic "incident" of the pontificate of Pope Francis developed from Rome's view of the involution of some aspects of Christianity in the United States, expressed in the now famous article by the editor of the Jesuit-run, Rome-based, and Vatican-vetted magazine *La Civiltà Cattolica*, Antonio Spadaro, and the editor of the Argentine edition of *L'Osservatore Romano*, Protestant theologian Marcelo Figueroa.[24] The article, published in July 2017 in Italian and in English and commented on widely in the United States, expressed the concerns of Catholic Rome—shared by many other Catholics in the United States and around the world—about the surge of a worldview of "us versus them" that made possible the development of a peculiar political ecumenism between Catholics and Protestants in the United States.[25] This ecumenism provided a

---

[23] See Antonio Spadaro and Diego Fares, "Il trittico americano di Francesco. Cuba, Stati Uniti e Messico, *La Civiltà Cattolica*, 3977 (March 12, 2016): 472–92.

[24] Antonio Spadaro and Marcelo Figueroa, "Evangelical Fundamentalism and Catholic Integralism: A Surprising Ecumenism," *La Civiltà Cattolica*, 4010 (July 13, 2017).

[25] For some reactions to the article by Spadaro and Figueroa in the United States, see Christoph R. Altieri, "Manichean Misdiagnosis," in *First Things* (July 18, 2017); Charles Chaput, "A Word about Useful Tools," in *Catholic News Agency* (July 18, 2017); Drew Christiansen, "Catholic-Evangelical Relations Are Richer than the Conspiracies Civilta Cattolica Described," in *America* (July 21, 2017); "The Religious

challenge not only to the US clerical hierarchies, but also to the other hierarchies—the political, intellectual, social, and financial hierarchies of the United States. It became almost official that the American experiment of the political-ideological ecumenism crafted during the "culture wars" was under review in Rome, where the "ecumenism of hate" was being contrasted with the "ecumenism of the frontiers" of Pope Francis.[26]

This particular ecumenism of Pope Francis expresses the geo-politics of the pontificate: the de-Europeanization of Catholicism has important consequences for the inclusion—theologically, culturally, politically—of non-European Catholicism, especially of Latin America, Africa, and Asia. There is a clear gap between the political ecumenism around the right-to-life and related issues in North America and the "ecumenism of blood" Pope Francis has talked about since the beginning of his pontificate, referring to the challenges for Christians—Catholics together with non-Catholics—in areas of the world where they are being persecuted. There is an ecumenical landscape that has changed tragically as a consequence of the wars that target religious mi-norities—Christians included—in Africa, the Middle East, and Asia. What Francis calls the "ecumenism of blood" is certainly part of his ecumenical outlook, as he said many times, especially in his December 14, 2013, interview with Andrea Tornielli in the Italian newspaper *La Stampa*.

Francis's ecumenism of blood is also a key aspect of Francis's geopolitics, which is tilted toward the southern hemisphere, the Near East, the Middle East, and Asia. It is a geo-theological map that began ecumenically with the patriarch of Constantinople in Turkey, with whom Francis established a very close relationship following the presence of Bartholomew at the inaugural mass of the new pope on March 19, 2013, and was cemented by the first meeting between Francis and Bartholomew at the Phanar during the pope's visit to Turkey, November 28–30, 2014.

Francis holds a geopolitics that does not shy away from dip-lomatic controversy, as we can see from the incident sparked

---

Right and Wrong," editorial, *Commonweal* (July 25, 2017); Michael Sean Winters, "The Civiltá Article: Finally!" *National Catholic Reporter* (July 14, 2017).

[26] Spadaro, "Sfida all'apocalisse," 40.

by the April 12, 2015, liturgy celebrated in Saint Peter's Square together with the Armenians for the one hundredth anniversary of the genocide (*genocide* is Francis's choice of word) of the Armenians at the hands of Turkey. The tensions between the Vatican and Turkey were revived one year later, when Francis visited Armenia, June 24–26, 2016. He talked about reconciliation in the region and on June 27 signed a joint declaration with the Catholicos Karekin II (supreme head of the Armenian Apostolic Church). The declaration speaks of "the continuing conflicts on ethnic, economic, political and religious grounds in the Middle East and other parts of the world" as well as the "de-sacralised and materialistic vision of man and the human family" and "the crisis of the family in many countries." Reconciliation, for Francis, also means ecclesial reconciliation, which is not without costs for the cohesion of individual churches, including Catholicism, as when Francis rejected "uniatism" as a viable path toward Christian unity today in an address to a delegation of the Moscow Patriarchate on May 30, 2018, hinting at the demands from the Greek Catholic Church in Ukraine to be established as a patriarchal church.

Church and Peace: Field Hospital for a Wounded World

The major difference between the Western and the Vatican perceptions of the world (and the Vatican's international activity) is in relation to the Middle East, the Arab world, and Africa. Francis's "geopolitics of mercy" pays particular attention to the forgotten areas of the world, where violence is systematic and endemic. The geopolitical vision of Francis is deeply spiritual: "the contemplation of God's face leads to thinking of reconciliation in the world as a realistic objective."[27]

The map of Francis's international trips draws a very clear picture of where Francis sees the need for the word of the Catholic Church to be present with the bishop of Rome. A few moments offer particularly clear examples, such as the decision to open the "holy door" of the Extraordinary Jubilee of Mercy in Bangui on November 29, 2015, during his trip to the Central

---

[27] Spadaro, "Sfida all'apocalisse," 25.

African Republic. A few months later, during his speech to the diplomatic corps in Rome on January 11, 2016, Francis reaffirmed the link between his trips and the need for reconciliation (Kenya, Uganda, and the Central African Republic; Bosnia and Herzegovina; Bolivia, Ecuador, and Paraguay; Cuba and the United States; Sri Lanka and the Philippines; Korea), but he also rejected the instrumentalization of religion by fundamentalists:

> Where God's name has been misused to perpetrate injustice, I wanted to reaffirm, together with the Muslim community of the Central African Republic, that "those who claim to believe in God must also be men and women of peace" and consequently of mercy, for one may never kill in the name of God. Only a distorted ideological form of religion can think that justice is done in the name of the Almighty by deliberately slaughtering defenseless persons, as in the brutal terrorist attacks which occurred in recent months in Africa, Europe and the Middle East.

Compared to his predecessors, Pope Francis has taken very high political risks for the ministry of the bishop of Rome as pope of the Catholic Church at the service of the cause of peace and reconciliation. This was particularly visible during his trip to the United Arab Emirates, February 3–5, 2019, with the joint signature on February 4 of the "Document for Human Fraternity for World Peace and Living Together" with the grand imam of Al-Azhar. The visit and the document represent a milestone in the history of Christian-Muslim dialogue in the effort to de-escalate interreligious tensions and to reject the use of religion for violence. It is also another chapter in the Catholic Church's effort to speak as an agent for peace. This could have long-term consequences on the pluri-centennial magisterial tradition of "just war." But Francis's contribution is especially a theological interpretation of war in the context of the recent history of the theological manipulation of God with the goal of waging war between religions. The Abu Dhabi statement implicitly looks at the "political manipulation of religions" as one of the signs of our time.

This relentless ministry of Francis for reconciliation has been a permanent aspect of his pontificate, which he continued with his trip to Egypt in April 2017, to Colombia in September 2017, and to Bangladesh and Myanmar in November–December 2017. Francis sought reconciliation among Christians of different confessions, Christians and Muslims, and different nations and ethnicities. In the trip to Bangladesh and Myanmar the pope went as far as advocating respect for a Muslim minority persecuted in a Buddhist-majority country like Myanmar. During the May 2014 trip to Israel, Francis stopped to pray at the Israeli separation wall in Bethlehem—a silent statement against a symbol of division and conflict between two peoples and two nations, but with evident religious implications.

Francis's action on the world map has not just been in "band-aiding" emergency situations where the word of the church can raise consciousness and restore dialogue toward peace and justice. It has been also a programmatic, intentional discourse, with a significant—even though not in a magisterially definitive way—impact on the Catholic Church's view on war and peace. On December 7, 2014, Francis sent a message to the Vienna Conference on the Humanitarian Impact of Nuclear Weapons that emphasized references to John XXIII's *Pacem in Terris* and to the pastoral constitution of Vatican II, *Gaudium et Spes*. In April 2016 a Vatican-hosted conference titled "Nonviolence and Just Peace," sponsored by the Vatican Dicastery for Justice and Peace and by the movement Pax Christi, moved more decidedly in its final document against and beyond the just war doctrine.[28] On September 20, 2017, the Holy See, also in the name of and on behalf of the Vatican City State, signed the Treaty on the Prohibition of Nuclear Weapons, adopted on July 7, 2017, at the end of the United Nations Conference aimed at negotiating a legally binding instrument to prohibit nuclear weapons. On October 1, 2017, during his visit to Bologna, Francis delivered an address, "Incontro con Gli Studenti e al Mondo Accademico" (not available in English), quoting two key moments in the history of the Catholic teaching on peace in the twentieth century, both with evident ties to the Catholic Church in Bologna: Benedict XV's appeal of November 1917 for the end of World War I,

---

[28] The final document of the conference was "crafted in a consensus process" and titled "An Appeal to the Catholic Church to Re-commit to the Centrality of Gospel Nonviolence" (April 2016).

and Cardinal Lercaro's homily against the bombings in Vietnam on January 1, 1968.

Besides the doctrine and practice of peace, Francis's pontificate has moved decisively to address a number of global issues that are typical of the international activity of the Holy See and the Catholic Church in the world of today, even though they do not concern Catholics only: religious freedom for all (for example, for the Muslim minority of the Rohingya in Myanmar); for the environment (for example, with the encyclical *Laudato Si'*); against human trafficking; and for an international order between the old order and the disruption caused by the crisis of globalization. The critique of the "technocratic paradigm" is the most synthetic definition of Francis's worldview. Pope Francis's political message is essentially about the attempt to save politics from functionalist, positivistic technocracy. This is Francis's junction with the emphasis of his predecessors on relativism, which the Jesuit pope sees in the context of the impact of modern globalized economy on the human person and its complex network of relations.[29] Francis's global action has repeatedly stressed the importance—in a striking paradox for the contemporary, post–Papal States Roman papacy—of a new primacy of politics for the common good. Francis's pontificate favors a distancing of the clergy and the ecclesiastical institutions from politics in order to avoid the instrumentalization of religion, but at the same time it is a pontificate that seeks the rehabilitation of politics at the international and global level. Francis sees a real danger for democracy in technocracy, and politics has a key role to play in this struggle.[30]

Global Papacy in an Age of Disruption

The actions of Francis's papacy are inseparable from the urgency of the social, cultural, and political consequences of the disruption caused by globalization. There is a parallel here with the papacy of one century before; the end of the First World War

---

[29] See Borghesi, *Jorge Mario Bergoglio*, 215.
[30] See Diego Fares, "Papa Francesco e la politica," *La Civiltà Cattolica*, 3976 (February 27, 2016): 373–86.

was one of the moments leading to important developments in Catholic teaching on key social issues. Francis's is the liminal papacy between different ages, especially from the point of view of the globalization of Christianity and Catholicism.

Some of his actions have followed the examples of his predecessors: the initiatives for Catholic global ecumenism (the trip to Lund in October 2016 for the beginning of the one hundredth anniversary of the Reformation) and global interreligious dialogue (the visit to Assisi in September 2016 for the thirtieth anniversary of the first World Day of Prayer for Peace in Assisi). The theology underlying the global initiatives of the papacy has not changed dramatically since his post–Vatican II predecessors. But the global context has changed dramatically from that early post–Vatican II period. In this sense it is not surprising that the most important successes of Francis's international activity have been in areas still marked by the geopolitics of the Cold War— or at least more marked by the twentieth century than by the disruption of the early twenty-first century: the normalization of the relations between the United States and Cuba in December 2014, and the Vatican opening to the People's Republic of China with the agreement of September 2018.

Geopolitically, the real success of Francis's papacy is the fact that his pontificate has clearly positioned Catholicism at odds with the responses to the disruption of globalization: Francis emphasizes the difference in the Catholic reading of the crisis and disruption of globalization. We can see the impact of the change of context for the message of Francis in three areas: his refusal to act as a "strongman,"[31] his emphasis on synodality, and his denunciation of the instrumentalization of religion for purposes of ethno-nationalism and tribalism.

Refusal to Act as a "Strongman"

Francis has continued the tradition of the post–World War II and post–Vatican II papacies of acting and speaking in favor of

---

[31] For the crisis of democracy and the dangers of populism looking for a political savior, see Pope Francis, "El peligro en tiempos de crisis es buscar un salvador que nos devuelva la identidad y nos defienda con muros," interview with *El País* [Spanish newspaper], January 22, 2017.

human rights and of democracy as a system compatible with the modern understanding of the dignity of the human person. The change of context is that until the end of the twentieth century, the discourses on globalization in the Catholic Church and in the Western system were, if not the same, largely overlapping, and this is no longer true today. The Catholic discourse on the chances given by internationalism and global networks for the flourishing of the human person had to deal not only with a more realistic perception, internally, of the ills of globalization (Francis's "globalization of indifference"), but especially with the calls, coming both from Catholic voices and from centers of political and cultural influence in the "Christian West," to disrupt internationalism and globalization.

On the other side of the geopolitical map, both the crisis of the Russian democracy and the conversion of China to a different kind of pro-capitalist communism have in mind a state-controlled religion that offers the papacy opportunities for dialogue as well as risks of being manipulated. Francis's open door to Putin's Russia—the three audiences with President Putin in November 2013, June 2015, and July 2019, and the meeting with Patriarch of Moscow Kirill in Cuba in February 2016—despite the Ukrainian crisis reveals the complexity of the international situation typical of this pontificate. Putin's attempt to make of the Orthodox Church an instrument of the neo-imperialist Russia ideology of the *Russkij Mir* (an expansionist idea of "Russian world") is at odds with Francis's post-Constantinian view of the relationship between the church and political power; at the same time, Russia continues to be a primary point of reference for the Roman papacy, both theologically and geopolitically.

The major difference now from the time of Ostpolitik between the 1960s and the 1980s is that the challenges against the church's message on democracy and human rights no longer come only from the "other," that is, the communist or the "religious other," but also from the Christian and Catholic world within the Western hemisphere.

Emphasis on Synodality and an Ecclesiology of the People

The pontificate of the ecclesiology of the people shows a second kind of gap with regard to world politics today: the difficult relationship with the ambiguities of populism (a term that has very different meanings and echoes in Latin America, in North America, and in Europe) and an encouragement to invest in participation in the institutions of the church as well as in the political sphere. Francis's emphasis on the church as a people is trying to lift up synodality as an antidote to populism—both political and ecclesial populism. But what Francis is trying to do with synodality also says something about the church's answer to the problem of representation in social and political bodies today. During the twentieth century, especially between World War II and Vatican II, the Catholic Church accepted intellectually the ideas of political, representative, and constitutional democracy. Today, Catholic ecclesiology and the institutional church are trying to see how much of modern efforts toward fair representation can become part of the institutional church. Francis is not afraid to let the people be active participants in the ecclesial process.

But there is a new problem today. The crisis, developing under our very eyes, of the idea of representation and of the ideal of secular, political democracy is having an impact on the church. The church is catching up with the democratic revolutions of the nineteenth and twentieth century only now, when democracy is being redefined by the virtual world of social media and social networks. Of course, representation in the church is not the same as democratization of the church. But a weakened culture of participation means also a weaker ability of the church to represent, that is, to make possible the effective presence of the Trinity through Christ and the Spirit. Undermining, in the name of an idiosyncratic idea of orthodox teaching, the legitimacy of the institutions that cooperate to the representation of Christ in the church means working toward an authoritarian-corporate or, on the other side of the spectrum, a populistic-demagogic system. Pope Francis's pontificate coincides with the end of the almost exclusive emphasis of the church's magisterium on the life issues and the biopolitics of the physical human body; it now has to deal with a vertical crisis of the "intermediate bodies" between the individual and power, in politics and in the economic system.

Denunciation of Ethno-Nationalism
and Tribalism Waged in the Name of Religion

The third and most visible challenge brought by Francis to world leaders has been in the denunciation of ethno-nationalism and tribalism waged in the name of religion. In his speeches to European leaders Francis has stepped back from the usual emphasis on the link between the European Union and the "Christian roots" of the continent. Instead, he has used the image of the roots as something that Christians today have to water and not shield as a possession. As he said May 6, 2016, at his acceptance of the Charlemagne Prize: "Only a Church rich in witnesses will be able to bring back the pure water of the Gospel to the roots of Europe. In this enterprise, the path of Christians towards full unity is a great sign of the times and a response to the Lord's prayer 'that they may all be one' (*Jn* 17:21)."

In the actual conditions of Europe at this time in his pontificate, Francis's message amounts to a criticism of the temptation to rebuild Europe as a fortress against migrants and refugees. The pope in Rome demonstrated that he was no fan of the dream of something like a neo-Hapsburg Catholic Europe, in which the new right-wing and populist governments of Italy, Austria, Poland, Hungary, and Slovenia (and of the "free state" of Bavaria in the federal republic of Germany) could build a front against globalization, Islam, and what they see as the destruction of European culture.

On May 2, 2019, Francis articulated his view of the crisis of globalization in a speech to the participants in the plenary session of the Pontifical Academy of Sciences:

The Church has always encouraged love of one's people, of country; respect for the value of various cultural expressions, uses and customs and for the just ways of living rooted in peoples. At the same time, the Church has admonished individuals, peoples and governments regarding deviations from this attachment when focused on exclusion and hatred of others, when it becomes hostile, wall-building nationalism, or even racism or anti-Semitism. The Church observes with concern the re-emergence, somewhat throughout the world, of aggressive tendencies toward foreigners, types of migrants, as well as that growing nationalism that disregards the common good.

Pope Francis is not a defender of the liberal order that brought in the neoliberal economic system. At the same time, Francis is also not an advocate of demagogic and simplistic solutions to the crisis of that order nationally and internationally, given the neo-nationalistic and xenophobic instincts of the anti-system and anti-establishment political parties. Francis's international actions amounted also to a rejection of the plan of Catholic traditionalism and anti-liberalism in America to take back Europe from secularism, multiculturalism, immigration, globalization, and, in particular, from the European Union. In this we see the connections between this global papacy and the anti-internationalist agenda, which is the agenda of the political opponents of this pontificate.

These opponents have a cultural and political capital in the United States. White evangelicalism and white Catholicism may tend toward the same conservative political parties, but they do not have the same cosmopolitan vision of the world. The Catholic Church has a global, internationalist, and cosmopolitan worldview that is fundamentally different from the agenda of neo-nationalists and nativists. Francis expresses a vision of citizenship, identity, and of the geographical position of a church that is universalist and internationalist, including in its perspective on interreligious issues, especially Islam.[32] White-Anglo evangelical Christianity does not express the same idea of citizenship in the world, either theologically or geopolitically, and this is one of the roots of the "prosperity gospel." The white-Anglo evangelical world represents and embodies the tendency toward the de-confessionalization of Christianity together with its ethnicization and tribalism—an extended phase in the crisis of the evangelical mind.[33]

---

[32] See Richard Cimino, "'No God in Common': American Evangelical Discourse on Islam after 9/11," *Review of Religious Research* 47, no. 2 (December 2005): 162–74.

[33] See Mark A. Noll, *The Scandal of the Evangelical Mind* (Grand Rapids, MI: Eerdmans, 1994).

A certain involution in the geopolitics of America and of American Christianity has an effect on the geopolitics of the Catholic pope. If it is true that the experience of the Argentine Bergoglio with the diversification of Christianity in Latin America, in which evangelicalism is growing, should bring Francis and the American evangelical world closer, we must take into account the crisis in the links between the churches of North America and Latin America—Catholic churches, but also non-Catholic and evangelical ones.

The Church and the World as a City, not a Village

There are at least four elements necessary for understanding the the geopolitical, historical, and ecclesial vision of Francis and its actions on the world map today.

The first element is that of a "Catholic Pangea" in movement: the global pontificate of Francis is characterized not only by a programmatic decentralization of Rome with respect to the global scenario, but also by the decentralization of other "centers"—including North America—moving toward becoming a church oriented toward the existential peripheries and the peripheries of the world. The Catholic Pangea describes the redefinition of distances and trajectories in the relations among the different geographical components of the Catholic world in their cultural, political, theological, and spiritual components. With respect to this, Francis places himself at the service of the church, listening to it without an agenda of authoritative interventions from above in either the doctrinal or political field. But letting go of the philosophical idea of an all-defining center of Catholicism has a great impact on a church that used to think of itself in terms of center—consciously or unconsciously, both in its conservative component (with its *reconquista* agenda against theological liberalism, against the pluralization of the religious world, and against the secular world) and its progressive aspect (with its agenda of universalization of same-sex marriage, of a feminist theology of women's empowerment, and of the theologization of identity politics).

A second element is that of a pontificate that has deep insights about the parallels and the convergences between the trajectories of the church and the world, according to the ecclesiology of *Gaudium et Spes* (1965). The history of the reception of Vatican II sees a first phase of ebullient embrace of the ecclesiology of the council, followed in the mid-1980s by a more skeptical view, if not a rejection, of the ecclesiology of the church *in the modern world*. Francis's activity in world affairs reflects a renewed engagement of the papacy with the ecclesiology of *Gaudium et Spes*, its emphasis on the pluralism of cultures, and the overcoming of the model of medieval Christendom for the church of today. But the world in which the church of Pope Francis operates is significantly more fragmented—theologically and politically—than the world at the time of Vatican II.

A third element of tension between the actions of Francis and of the world of today, and of the West especially, is the imaginary about the role of the human element in a world dealing with the epochal crisis of migrants and refugees. For Francis as a priest, a Jesuit, and a bishop close to migrants and refugees, the church and the world are in a process of global "resettlement." If the American imagination is that of a world for settlers, a world to be colonized by colonizers, for Francis it is a world for *re*-settlers, for the displaced, in which the languages of identity and force must be replaced by a language of dialogue and mercy. This entails a profound and critical reexamination of Christian culture and Christianity in relationship to the Western identity.

Finally, the fourth element of tension has to do with the radical difference between the North American and the Latin American religious worlds in their relationship with the urban and megalopolitan worlds with respect to the rural world. Francis speaks of the world as a global city, in which God and faith live in a complex and multifaceted, multicultural, and multi-religious environment, crossed by the secular and composite identity.[34] The social and religious imagination of Francis is essentially urban, cosmopolitan, and pluralist, different from a social and religious imaginary where the city is essentially secularist, dominated by the abandonment of God. On the contrary, Francis sees the urbanization of religious life as a challenge and an opportunity for

---

[34] See Carlos Maria Galli, *Dio vive in città. Verso una nuova pastorale urbana* (Vatican City: Libreria Editrice Vaticana, 2014).

the church; Francis's imagination of a Christian community does not take place in an ethnically or culturally homogenous village or frontier to be conquered and defended from external assaults, especially from pluralism and from the secular.[35]

---

[35] See Massimo Faggioli, *Catholicism and Citizenship: Political Cultures of the Church in the Twenty-First Century* (Collegeville, MN: Liturgical Press, 2017), 123–48.

Conclusion

This brief exploration of the ecclesiology of globalization and its pastoral and theological application in Pope Francis's papacy attempts to offer a few insights into the role of Jorge Mario Bergoglio as bishop of Rome in the centuries-long process of transformation of the Roman Catholic Church in an inculturated and decentralized global Catholic Church.

This is not a book on global Catholicism or a book on ecclesiology for a global church. The scope of this book is not only more narrow, but also more mindful of a pontificate in full development, especially with regard to the relations between the Vatican and geographically and theologically distant areas of the Catholic communion (for example, the special bishops' synod for the region of the Amazon, October 6–27, 2019) and with regard to the relations with other religions (for example, the trips to Abu Dhabi and to Morocco of February and March 2019). The consequences of the acts that have received priority from Pope Francis will have to be evaluated in the long term, beyond the short-lived news cycle that now tends to shape more and more the narratives on the church. The liminal nature of Francis's pontificate has to do also with temporal liminality; the long-term perspective will thus be necessary for understanding the trajectories of Catholic globalization.

This is also because Francis's papacy was made possible by Benedict XVI's resignation. Francis's papacy has coincided institutionally with the departure from the rule of papacy for life—something that has been, in its monarchical and imperial feature, inseparable from the mystique of the papal office. Pope Francis's pontificate is a particularly important step in the biography of a particular man, Jorge Mario Bergoglio, but possibly not the last step, as it used to be for popes who never had resignation as a realistic choice. The spiritual and theological evolution that the election to the papacy meant for Francis could bear fruit somewhere else, outside the Vatican, in case the 266th successor of Peter decides to resign. What is certain is that Francis's global Catholic identity cannot be understood without a comparison between his biography and his predecessors' and without locating his pontificate in the historical context of the Catholic Church, that is, what this pontificate represents in the history of the papacy.

This provides keys for understanding Francis's reception of Vatican II as the council that realized and acknowledged—more intuitively than consciously—the global nature of Catholicism in the one human family: Francis's particular relations with the many peripheries the global Catholic Church today comprises, in particular with North America; Francis's style of governance of the Catholic Church; and his leadership as the most authoritative representative on the world stage of a global religious community.

The global dimension of the pontificate is essential not only for understanding Francis, but also for understanding the opposition to his pontificate. Much of the attention given to Francis revolves around the opposition against him, not due to the loudness of this opposition, or its tactics, or the fact that it relied on well-organized and well-funded Catholic circles literally claiming to be "more Catholic than the pope." Rather, the theological, institutional, and political opposition against Francis reveals the scope of this pontificate and the central importance of its understanding of globalization.

There is certainly an opposition that derives from the particular effect on the church of the pontificate of his predecessor, whose role in the church must be considered in light of his long tenure (almost a quarter of a century) as prefect of the Congregation for the Doctrine of the Faith during the pontificate of John Paul II. There is also an opposition that has become more visible thanks to the growing influence of social media on the new ecclesial cybernetics shaped by the virtualization of religious identities.

But there also is a genuine and original opposition to Francis that has to do with his focus on the peripheries. The opposition to Pope Francis is made up of different streams. There is a *theological* opposition that is nostalgic of a supposedly unchanging and immutable John Paul II–Benedict XVI paradigm. Then there is an *institutional* opposition that is trying to defend the ecclesiastical status quo. Finally, there is a *social-political* opposition that is concerned with the political, economic, and ideological sustainability of the Roman Catholic Church after a pontificate that is radically on the side of the poor, a fear that Francis's global Catholicism could be disastrous for Western civilization and for Catholicism as a Western religion.

All these different kinds of opposition have to do with Francis's vision of a global Catholic Church. If the defining shift during the early post–Vatican II period, from *Humanae Vitae* on, was the eruption of the biopolitical issue, the defining issue of this second post–Vatican II period is the globalization of Catholicism amid the crisis of globalization itself. We are undergoing still another major shift, one from the biopolitical perspective to the perspectives of the global south, which are necessary for understanding the complexity of Roman Catholicism today.

This book does not rely on one particular set of strong assumptions about the theological essence of the papal office, one of the ministries that has proven most mutable and adaptive to circumstances in church history. One strong assumption, though, is that the papacy is necessary for the global Catholic Church and that it is necessary to look at Catholicism as *a world* more than as *just a church*. Catholicism is not just a set of doctrines and rules, of texts and traditions. The church coexists with and insists on a territory that is the globe, and it has claims on and representations of the world that have defied and dealt with empires, nations, and totalitarian ideologies. The challenges brought to the church by empires, nations, and totalitarian ideologies have redefined Catholicism and its relationship with the world. The popes always have had a key role in shaping but also in interpreting the church's response to those challenges. Now is the time to look at how globalization and the papacy are interacting. The pontificate of Francis has proven to be a particularly telling and decisive moment in this new page in the history of the Catholic Church.

Bibliography

Abbott, Walter M., ed. *The Documents of Vatican II*. London: Chapman, 1966.

Alberigo, Giuseppe, ed. *History of Vatican II*. 5 volumes. In English, Joseph A. Komonchak, ed. Maryknoll, NY: Orbis Books, 1995–2006.

Banchoff, Thomas, and José Casanova, eds. *The Jesuits and Globalization: Historical Legacies and Contemporary Challenges*. Washington, DC: Georgetown University Press, 2016.

Batlogg, Andreas R. *Der Evangelische Papst. Hält Franziskus, was er verspricht?* Munich: Kösel, 2018.

Beozzo, José Oscar. *Pacto das catacumbas. Por uma Igreja servidora e pobre*. São Paulo: Paulinas, 2015.

Bevans, Stephen B. "Decree on the Church's Missionary Activity," in Stephen B. Bevans and Jeffrey Gros, *Evangelization and Religious Freedom*: Ad Gentes, Dignitatis Humanae. Mahwah, NJ: Paulist Press, 2009, 3–148.

Bier, Georg. "Papa Francesco legislatore," *Il Regno–Attualità* 22 (2017): 682–85.

Borghesi, Massimo. *Jorge Mario Bergoglio. Una biografia intellettuale*. Milan: Jaca Book, 2017. In English, Massimo Borghesi, *The Mind of Pope Francis: The Intellectual Journey of Jorge Mario Bergoglio*. Translated by Barry Hudock. Collegeville MN: Liturgical Press, 2018.

Boschini, Paolo. "Il ritorno dello *zoon politikon*. L'antropologia politica di *Evangelii Gaudium*," *Rivista di Teologia dell'Evangelizzazione* 22, no. 44 (July–December 2018): 335–55.

Casanova, José. "The Jesuits through the Prism of Globalization, Globalization through a Jesuit Prism." In *The Jesuits and*

Globalization: Historical Legacies and Contemporary Challenges, ed. Thomas Banchoff and José Casanova, 261–85. Washington, DC: Georgetown University Press, 2016.

Catto, Michela, and Claudio Ferlan, eds. *I gesuiti e i papi*. Bologna: Il Mulino, 2015.

Chiron, Jean-François. "Sensus fidei et vision de l'Église chez le Pape François," *Recherches de Science Religieuses* 2 (2016) (tome 104): 187–205.

Cozzi, Alberto, Roberto Repole, and Giannino Piana, eds. *Papa Francesco. Quale teologia*. Afterword by Cardinal Gianfranco Ravasi. Assisi: Cittadella, 2016.

Cuda, Emilce. *Leggere Francesco. Teologia, etica e politica*. Preface by Juan Carlos Scannone. Turin: Bollati Boringhieri, 2018. Original: Buenos Aires: Manantial, 2016.

Dianich, Severino. *Magistero in movimento. Il caso papa Francesco*. Bologna: EDB, 2016.

Eckholt, Margit. *An die Peripherie gehen. In der Spuren des armen Jesus. Vom Zweiten Vatikanum zu Papst Franziskus*. Ostfildern: Grünewald, 2015.

Faggioli, Massimo. *Catholicism and Citizenship: Political Cultures of the Church in the Twenty-First Century*. Collegeville, MN: Liturgical Press, 2017.

———. *A Council for the Global Church: Receiving Vatican II in History*. Minneapolis: Fortress Press, 2015.

———. *Pope Francis: Tradition in Transition*. Mahwah, NJ: Paulist Press, 2015.

———. *The Rising Laity: Ecclesial Movements since Vatican II*. Mahwah, NJ: Paulist Press, 2016.

———. *Sorting Out Catholicism: Brief History of the New Ecclesial Movements*. Collegeville, MN: Liturgical Press, 2014.

———. *True Reform: Liturgy and Ecclesiology in* Sacrosanctum Concilium. Collegeville, MN: Liturgical Press, 2012.

———. *Vatican II: The Battle for Meaning*. Mahwah, NJ: Paulist Press, 2012.

———. *Il vescovo e il concilio. Modello episcopale e aggiornamento al Vaticano II*. Bologna: Il Mulino, 2005.

Fares, Diego. "A dieci anni da Aparecida. Alle fonti del pontificato di Francesco," *La Civiltà Cattolica*, 4006 (May 20, 2017): 338–52.

———. "Papa Francesco e la politica," *La Civiltà Cattolica*, 3976 (February 27, 2016): 373–86.

Fernández, Víctor Manuel, with Paolo Rodari. *Il progetto di Francesco. Dove vuole portare la chiesa*. Bologna: EMI, 2014.

Forestier, Luc. "Le pape François et la synodalité. *Evangelii Gaudium*, nouvelle étape dans la réception de Vatican II," *Nouvelle revue théologique* 137, no. 4 (October 2015): 597–614.

Froehle, Bryan T., and Mary L. Gautier. *Global Catholicism: Portrait of a World Church*. Maryknoll, NY: Orbis Books, 2003.

Gaillardetz, Richard R. *Ecclesiology for a Global Church: A People Called and Sent*. Maryknoll, NY: Orbis Books, 2008.

Galavotti, Enrico. "Il Concilio di papa Francesco." In *Il Conclave e papa Francesco. Il primo anno di pontificato*, ed. Alberto Melloni, 35–69. Rome: Istituto della Enciclopedia Italiana, 2014.

———. "Jorge Mario Bergoglio e il concilio Vaticano II: fonte e metodo," *Rivista di Teologia dell'Evangelizzazione* 22 , no. 43 (2018): 61–88.

Galli, Carlos Maria. *Dio vive in città. Verso una nuova pastorale urbana*. Vatican City: Libreria Editrice Vaticana, 2014.

Graziano, Manlio. *In Rome We Trust: The Rise of Catholics in American Political Life*. Stanford, CA: Stanford University Press, 2017. Original in Italian: *In Rome We Trust. L'ascesa dei cattolici nella vita politica degli Stati Uniti*. Bologna: Il Mulino, 2016.

Hünermann, Peter, and Bernd Jochen Hilberath, eds. *Herders theologischer Kommentar zum Zweiten Vatikanischen Konzil*. 5 volumes. Freiburg i.B.: Herder, 2004–5.

Ivereigh, Austen. *The Great Reformer: Francis and the Making of a Radical Pope*. New York: Holt, 2014.

Lafont, Ghislain. *Piccolo saggio sul tempo di papa Francesco*. Bologna: EDB, 2017.

Luciani, Rafael. *El papa Francisco y la teología del pueblo*. Madrid: PPC, 2016. In English, *Pope Francis and the Theology of the People*. Maryknoll, NY: Orbis Books, 2017.

Mannion, Gerard, ed. *Pope Francis and the Future of Catholicism*: Evangelii Gaudium *and the Papal Agenda*. New York: Cambridge University Press, 2017.

McGreevy, John T. *American Jesuits and the World: How an Embattled Religious Order Made Modern Catholicism Global*. Princeton, NJ: Princeton University Press, 2016.

Melloni, Alberto. *Il Giubileo. Una storia*. Rome-Bari: Laterza, 2015.

Menozzi, Daniele. *I papi e il moderno. Una lettura del cattolicesimo contemporaneo (1903–2016)*. Brescia: Morcelliana, 2016.

Miccoli, Giovanni. *Fra mito della cristianità e secolarizzazione. Studi sul rapporto chiesa-società nell'età contemporanea*. Genoa: Marietti, 1985.

Morra, Stella. *Dio non si stanca. La Misericordia come forma ecclesiale*. Bologna: EDB, 2015.

Nacke, Stefan. *Die Kirche der Weltgesellschaft. Das II. Vatikanische Konzil und die Globalisierung des Katholizismus*. Wiesbaden: VS Verlag, 2010.

O'Malley, John W. *Vatican I: The Council and the Making of the Ultramontane Church*. Cambridge, MA: Belknap Press of Harvard University Press, 2018.

———. *What Happened at Vatican II*. Cambridge, MA: Belknap Press of Harvard University, 2008.

Piqué, Elisabetta. *Francesco. Vita e rivoluzione*. Turin: Lindau, 2013. Original in Spanish: Editorial El Ateneo, 2013. In English, *Pope Francis: Life and Revolution*. Chicago: Loyola Press, 2014.

Politi, Marco. *Pope Francis among the Wolves: The Inside Story of a Revolution*. Translated by William McCuaig. New York: Columbia University Press, 2015. Original in Italian: Rome-Bari: Laterza, 2014.

Prodi, Paolo. "Europe in the Age of Reformations: The Modern State and Confessionalization," *Catholic Historical Review* 103, no. 1 (Winter 2017): 1–19.

———. *Il paradigma tridentino. Un'epoca della storia della Chiesa*. Brescia: Morcelliana, 2010.

Quisinsky, Michael. "Prolegomena einer Theologie als Lebenswissenschaft 'auf der Grenze.' Papst Franziskus und die theologische Erkenntnislehre," *Theologie und Glaube* 107 (2017): 137–56.

Rahner, Karl. "Basic Theological Interpretation of the Second Vatican Council." In Karl Rahner, *Concern for the Church.* New York: Crossroad, 1981.

Riccardi, Andrea. *Periferie. Crisi e novità per la Chiesa.* Milan: Jaca Book, 2016. In English, *To the Margins: Pope Francis and the Mission of the Church.* Maryknoll, NY: Orbis Books, 2018.

———. *La sorpresa di papa Francesco. Crisi e futuro della Chiesa.* Milan: Mondadori, 2013.

Riccardi, Andrea, ed. *Il cristianesimo al tempo di papa Francesco.* Rome-Bari: Laterza, 2018.

Rubin, Sergio, and Francesca Ambrogetti. *El Jesuita. Conversaciones con el cardenal Jorge Bergoglio, sj.* Buenos Aires: Vergara-Grupo Zeta, 2010.

Ruggieri, Giuseppe. *Chiesa sinodale.* Rome-Bari: Laterza, 2017.

Rush, Ormond. *The Vision of Vatican II: Its Fundamental Principles.* Collegeville, MN: Liturgical Press, 2019.

Scaramuzzi, Iacopo. *Tango Vaticano. La Chiesa al tempo di Francesco.* Rome: Edizioni dell'Asino, 2015.

Schickendantz, Carlos. "Un enfoque empírico-teológico. En el método, el secreto de Medellín," *Teologia y Vida* 58, no. 4 (2017): 421–45.

———. "¿Una transformación metodológica inadvertida? La novedad introducida por *Gaudium et Spes* en los escritos de Joseph Ratzinger," *Teología y Vida* 57, no. 1 (2016): 9–37.

Schloesser, Stephen R. "'Dancing on the Edge of the Volcano': Biopolitics and What Happened after Vatican II," in *From Vatican II to Pope Francis: Charting a Catholic Future,* ed. Paul Crowley, SJ. Maryknoll, NY: Orbis Books, 2014.

Sedmak, Clemens. *A Church of the Poor: Pope Francis and the Transformation of Orthodoxy.* Maryknoll, NY: Orbis Books, 2016.

Sequeri, Pierangelo. *La cruna dell'ego. Uscire dal monoteismo del sé.* Milan: Vita e Pensiero, 2017.

————. "Il grembo famigliare dell'amore Chiesa e famiglia nell'*Amoris Laetitia*," *La Rivista del Clero Italiano* 1 (2017): 6–18.

Spadaro, Antonio. "'Amoris Laetitia.' Struttura e significato dell'Esortazione Apostolica post-sinodale di papa Francesco," *La Civiltà Cattolica*, 3980 (April 2, 2016): 105–28.

————, ed. *Il nuovo mondo di Francesco. Come il Vaticano sta cambiando la politica globale*. Padua: Marsilio, 2018.

————. "Intervista a Papa Francesco," *La Civiltà Cattolica*, 3918 (September 19, 2013): 449–77. In English, "A Big Heart Open to God," *America*, September 19, 2013.

————. "Lo sguardo di Magellano. L'Europa, Papa Francesco, e il Premio Carlo Magno," *La Civiltà Cattolica*, 3983 (June 11, 2016): 469–79.

Spadaro, Antonio, and Diego Fares. "Il trittico americano di Francesco. Cuba, Stati Uniti e Messico, *La Civiltà Cattolica* I, 3977 (March 12, 2016): 472–92.

Spadaro, Antonio, and Marcelo Figueroa. "Evangelical Fundamentalism and Catholic Integralism: A Surprising Ecumenism," *La Civiltà Cattolica*, 4010 (July 13, 2017): 105–10.

Spadaro, Antonio, and Carlos Maria Galli, eds. *For a Missionary Reform of the Church: The Civiltà Cattolica Seminar*. Translated by Demetrio S. Yocum. Foreword by Massimo Faggioli. Mahwah, NJ: Paulist Press, 2017. Original in Italian: *La riforma e le riforme nella chiesa*. Brescia: Queriniana, 2016.

————. *La riforma e le riforme nella chiesa*. Brescia: Queriniana, 2016.

Theobald, Christoph. *Accéder à la source*, vol. 1 in *La réception du concile Vatican II*. Paris: Cerf, 2009.

————. "L'exhortation apostolique *Evangelii Gaudium*. Esquisse d'une interprétation originale du Concile Vatican II," *Revue Théologique de Louvain* 46 (2015): 321–40.

————. *Fraternità. Il nuovo stile della Chiesa secondo papa Francesco*. Preface by Enzo Bianchi. Bose: Qiqajon, 2016.

————. *Urgences pastorales. Comprendre, partager, reformer*. Paris: Bayard, 2017.

Turina, Isacco. "Centralized Globalization: The Holy See and Human Mobility since World War II," *Critical Research on Religion* 3, no. 2 (2015): 189–205.

Vallely, Paul. *Pope Francis: The Struggle for the Soul of Catholicism.* New York: Bloomsbury, 2015.

Vergottini, Marco. *Il cristiano testimone. Congedo dalla teologia del laicato.* Bologna: EDB, 2017.

Vian, Giovanni. "Le Pape François et la mondialisation. Un pontificat pour un christianisme global?" In *Le pontificat romaine dans l'epoque contemporaine*, ed. Giovanni Vian. Venice: Università Ca' Foscari, 2018.

Index